ChatGPT Money Guide

Discover The Secrets to Making Money
Quickly and Easily with ChatGPT
(Beginners Guide)

© Copyright 2023 - All rights reserved.

The content contained within this book may not be reproduced, duplicated or transmitted without direct written permission from the author or the publisher.

Under no circumstances will any blame or legal responsibility be held against the publisher, or author, for any damages, reparation, or monetary loss due to the information contained within this book. Either directly or indirectly.

Legal Notice:

This book is copyright protected. This book is only for personal use. You cannot amend, distribute, sell, use, quote or paraphrase any part, or the content within this book, without the consent of the author or publisher.

Disclaimer Notice:

Please note the information contained within this document is for educational and entertainment purposes only. All effort has been executed to present accurate, up to date, and reliable, complete information. No warranties of any kind are declared or implied. Readers acknowledge that the author is not engaging in the rendering of legal, financial, medical or professional advice. The content within this book has been derived from various sources. Please consult a licensed professional before attempting any techniques outlined in this book.

By reading this document, the reader agrees that under no circumstances is the author responsible for any losses, direct or indirect, which are incurred as a result of the use of the information contained within this document, including, but not limited to, — errors, omissions, or inaccuracies.

Your Free Gift

As a way of saying thanks for your purchase, I'm offering a ChatGPT QuickStart Guide for FREE to my readers!

To get instant access just visit:

gptpenguin.com

Inside this QuickStart Guide you will discover:

- Step-by-step guide on how to get started with ChatGPT
- 33 Different Ways You Can Make Money Online
- Printable Income Tracker
- And so much more

If you want to learn how to get started with ChatGPT, make sure to grab the free QuickStart Guide.

TABLE OF CONTENTS

Introduction 1

Chapter 1: Setting The Foundations For Financial Success 4

Chapter 2: Making Money With Content Creation That You Need To Know 18

Chapter 3: Level Up Your Content Marketing With ChatGPT 41

Chapter 4: How ChatGPT Is Changing The Social Media Marketing Game 73

Chapter 5: How To Supercharge Productivity As A Freelancer 101

Chapter 6: ChatGPT And Its Alternatives 117

Conclusion 138

Introduction

A recent Forbes report revealed that 7 out of the top 10 fastest-growing online earners in 2023 used ChatGPT as their primary income source, despite many of them having never made money online before—a truly astounding statistic. The number of millionaires created through ChatGPT has grown by an astonishing 900% in the past year alone as more and more individuals with no experience tap into this incredible money-making opportunity!

What if you could join the thousands of ChatGPT users who have successfully generated a full-time income online, with some users even reporting earnings of up to $20,000 per month, all without any prior experience?

ChatGPT has the power to transform lives by unlocking the door to financial freedom for those in search of a sustainable income source. Its innovative technology and user-friendly interface make it accessible to people from all walks of life, regardless of their background or experience.

Are you yearning for financial freedom and a more fulfilling lifestyle?

So, if you're tired of trading your time for money and want to escape your 9-5 job, or if you want to achieve the perfect work-life balance by generating consistent earnings while enjoying quality time with your loved ones, or if you're a student who wants to focus on your studies while having a reliable monthly income without sacrificing your social life.

Then, this book is just for you, I'm going to walk you through step by step on how to make money on the internet the easiest way possible. There is virtually no ceiling on how much money you can make, ChatGPT is one of the most profitable ways to earn money online while sitting comfortably on your couch.

The allure of easy money has piqued the interest of many, TikTok user, IshTheCeo, charges companies up to $1000 for content generated by ChatGPT, effectively replacing traditional writers. IshTheCeo suggests that with this AI-powered tool, anyone can craft engaging stories and sell them to businesses.

If you haven't been living under a rock, you would know what ChatGPT is. You can become a millionaire just by using ChatGPT, I guarantee it. Every day, I receive heartfelt messages from individuals who have discovered a newfound sense of financial freedom and independence, all thanks to the training I provide in harnessing the power of ChatGPT. In this book, I will share the very same training that has transformed countless lives and enabled people to break free from the constraints of their 9-5 jobs. The strategies I reveal are accessible and straightforward, ensuring that anyone can achieve success with ease.

Through the pages of this book, you'll find a treasure trove of tips, tricks, and actionable steps designed to help you leverage ChatGPT to its fullest potential. The guidance I offer is grounded in real-world experience, backed by the countless success stories of those who have applied these methods and created thriving income streams. I genuinely believe that this information has the power to change your life, just as it has for so many others.

What sets this book apart is its focus on practical, step-by-step guidance that simplifies the process of making money online with

ChatGPT. I have distilled the essence of my knowledge into easily digestible chapters, ensuring that you can start implementing the strategies right away and begin to see tangible results. This is not just another book filled with empty promises; it is a roadmap to success, providing the tools you need to build a prosperous online business.

The power of ChatGPT is immense, and my mission is to make this revolutionary technology accessible to everyone, regardless of background or experience. By breaking down barriers and demystifying the process of generating income online, you will be empowered to take control of your financial future and create a life that you truly love. The time has come to step into your potential and embrace the possibilities that lie ahead.

So, are you ready to embark on this life-changing journey? Join the ranks of those who have already found success and happiness by following the guidance laid out in this book. Let me show you how to unlock the incredible potential of ChatGPT and create a sustainable, profitable income that can transform your life for the better. Don't wait another moment, dive in and discover the wealth of opportunities that await you! **—your bank account will thank you later!**

Chapter 1
Setting the Foundations For Financial Success

In today's fast-paced digital era, opportunities for financial freedom are closer than you think. Imagine waking up each day, leisurely sipping your coffee, and watching as your bank account swells with passive income, all from the comfort of your own home. This is no mere daydream; in this chapter, I will be unveiling the secrets of making money online, where you'll learn to tap into the goldmine of remote work and master the art of generating passive income.

Since we're talking about money, firstly more people should do it and secondly because money is such a massive source of stress in most of our lives, we often feel like we don't have enough of it and most of us trade more than 80 thousand hours of our lives; a huge chunk of our short time on this earth to go to work so we can make money which we need to live.

So, let's break it down! Basically, there are three stages to making money online but before delving into them, we have to know about what money actually is. In fact, there is a poem from the early 1900's that goes as follows...

Money is a matter of functions four
A medium, a measure, a standard, a store

And so, putting this all together at its core,

Money is just a medium for exchanging value. As we all use money to buy things, we find valuable. If we want to make money online, we need to provide value that someone else is willing to pay for. So, finding niches that are in demand is the key to making money with ChatGPT. In fact, you don't even need a massive budget to succeed in lucrative markets as ChatGPT's cost-effective solutions will have you soaring high without breaking the bank. It can lend a hand and make your journey to success in high-value niches smoother and more enjoyable.

Stage 1: Make Money Online by Selling Your Services

This is the easiest way of making money online as there are only two things you need to do:

1. Develop a skill that people are willing to pay for
2. Find people who are willing to pay for that skill

Step one includes developing a skill that others are willing to pay for. If you're thinking that you don't have any valuable skills, don't worry as you have the internet and you can learn online courses and pretty much anything online for free.

If you just look on the websites Fiverr or Upwork and browse their categories there are thousands of different things that people will pay you money for, ranging from coding, graphic design, illustrations to other things like writing, copy-writing, data entry and even being a personal assistant, there is a whole world of different things you can do on the internet, wherever you are in the world, as long as you have a reasonable internet connection.

Step two: find people who will pay you money for that skill or service. Now there are two sorts of people who will pay you for your services essentially. There are people in real life or people on the internet. You can find people in real life by referral links, building your brand and promoting your services offline.

Alternatively, you can find people to pay you for your services over the Internet. Personally, I've got my start on Upwork where people would post projects saying they need a web designer or a developer to do various things and I would bid on those projects and offer a really low price for around $10, $20, $30 and overtime as I got better, I started to charge more and more especially since I was starting to get decent reviews and building up a portfolio of the services I was offering.

However, after a few years, I realized that ultimately what I was doing was trading my time for money and that's ultimately not a very scalable model because our time is limited.

And so, if you want to make money online fast then we want to get to Stage 2.

Stage 2: Make Money Online by Selling Products

When you start selling products like physical or digital goods, your ability to make money online magnifies a lot because it's scalable. As it's not directly tied to the amount of time, you're putting in. We could sell pretty much anything online but the ideal product that we want to sell is something that has a one-time cost of time or money to make.

We can sell infinite copies of a product and ideally, we want the cost of reproduction to be zero and the cost of distribution to be zero, the ongoing time commitment to be as low as possible so we can make the thing once and then we can sell it like a million times without having to spend much more time.

So, the ideal product category then is digital goods or digital products. Now a digital good is anything from a website to an app or an online course or an e-book. All of these things have a one-time cost of production, a zero cost of reproduction, zero cost of distribution and hopefully a zero cost of maintenance as well.

So, we can either sell digital or physical products and there are basically two ways of selling it, either by selling other people's products or by selling our own products.

Stage 2 Beginner Level: Selling Other People's Products

There are various different ways of doing this but just to simplify the two that we're going to talk about are;

1. Drop shipping
2. Affiliate marketing

Drop shipping:

With drop shipping the basic idea is that we make a website selling bags, let's say for $40 a piece. When a customer orders that bag, we buy it from a third party that's actually selling the bag and we arrange for them to ship it to the customer so we're making $20 without ever handling the bag at all.

Affiliate Marketing:

Affiliate marketing is when you're selling someone else's stuff but you're getting a commission from each sale. For example, there is a review website called wirecutter and they do reviews about the best electronics in different categories and they have Amazon affiliate links. So, when someone clicks on that link and buys from Amazon then after deduction from the website, you will get around 1% to 3% commission on that sale. And if you get enough visitors buying products you can make a lot of money from affiliate marketing.

So that is how affiliate marketing works. You're selling someone else's stuff but you're getting a percentage commission on the sale. Now, let's get to the holy grail of making money online.

And the Holy Grail is Stage 2 Advanced Level!

Stage 2 Advanced Level: Selling Your Own Products

Stage 2 Advanced Level is when we're selling our own products. If we're selling our own stuff then we control everything from the aesthetics to the price to the distribution to the logistics and the entire customer experience we are controlling ourselves.

So, at this Stage there are three broad categories of products that you could sell:

1. Physical Products: you could try selling physical products. However, it's quite hard selling a physical product as it demands a lot of work. You have to manufacture it, distribute it, organize logistics which costs a lot of money. I wouldn't recommend doing the physical product thing as it is more trouble than it's probably worth.

2. Online Products: you could make a website or an app and you could sell access to that. For example, let's say you make an IOS game or something and people buy it from the app store you're making money off of that. Or let's say you're making a website that's offering some kind of service and you're charging people a subscription fee or something for access to that service.

3. Sell Educational Products: you can create educational products like eBooks or digital downloads or online courses because if you can teach something and you can teach it in a compelling and interesting way online, you will find that people are willing to pay you for that online education, as more and more people are turning to online education.

Even if you're an absolute beginner, you can teach other beginners. So, if you're thinking of making money online, you can easily sign up to a free trial of skill share and then you could watch videos in any category you like. And then you can make an online class teaching that skill to other people and if you want, you can sell it through your own website or if you want you can sell it through Udemy course or a skill share.

There are all sorts of different platforms that you can sell your expertise on and as long as it's good because we make money online by providing value. If it's valuable then people will buy it.

But as you might be thinking, we still need to find people who are willing to part with their hard-earned cash to buy what we're trying to sell them and that's where Stage 3 comes in.

Stage 3: Supercharge Your Money-Making Powers with Attention

There are various ways that you can get your product in front of people. You can:

- Run Facebook or Instagram ads
- Go around knocking on doors in your neighborhood
- Send cold emails to mailing lists

but really the easiest way of selling anything online is by grabbing attention.

and that's the attention of people who know, like and trust you.

and by far the easiest way of getting people to know, like and trust you is by providing valuable content on the Internet completely free of charge.

For example, you can start a blog about productivity tips and every week you could write one or two blog posts sharing your favorite productivity from books, academic papers, articles, podcasts and even your own life. Over time, if you do this consistently and provide value because again this is an exchange of value, we all care about. There is no shortcut to making money online besides you're providing value for free across the internet over a long period of time and then in three years' time you build up a mailing list of 20,000 people.

Now when you want to run your own productivity course you've got this mailing list of 20,000 people who know like and trust you from the value that you've given them for free over an extended period of time and now, they're far more likely to buy your thing and you've got an audience of people that you can sell to.

There is this marketing guy, Gary Vaynerchuk, who has this book called Jab Jab Jab right hook and the model for that is that a jab, it's kind of a boxing analogy. A jab is when you give someone content and valuable content for free and a right hook is when you ask them for something or try to sell them something and he said in an interview that actually he wished he could have called the book jab… 25 times and then right hook because that's the ratio of how free content versus paid content needs to be. You need to be providing 25 pieces of valuable free content for every right hook that you're launching every time you're asking someone to buy stuff.

I've been following people like Tim Ferriss who modeled this perfectly over time by just flooding the market with tons of valuable free content not really worrying about trying to charge people for things and then later on you know once you've got this audience of people who know like and trust you and would be interested in buying things from you.

So if you can build up that personal brand and that professional reputation. That audience of people that know, like and trust you at that point you are supercharging your abilities to make money online because now you can sell products, now you can sell services and in fact you can even sell attention directly by doing sponsorships and stuff like that.

There's a guy called Kevin Kelly who wrote a famous essay ages ago called 1,000 true fans where if you can just get a thousand people following you on the internet and those are your true fans. Let's say you're a musician they're the people who will go to every show, they'll buy the special edition of your album, if you can get a thousand people who like you enough to potentially pay you $100 a year for the stuff that you make, you're making $100,000 a year and you've got a full time living from a thousand true fans. So, the audience doesn't need to be that big but the way of building any kind of audience as Gary Vaynerchuk and Tim Ferriss say is to just produce a ton of valuable free content over a long period of time.

So, the point here is, you can make money online by giving away content for free for an extended period of time and building an audience. After that you can sell them your skill or services and make money online through selling products, services and attention online. Trust me, you can make much more than you do from your 40-80 hours job a week.

How To Choose the Right Money-Making Method

Choosing the right online money-making method depends on your skills, interests, and lifestyle. To help you make the best decision, follow these steps:

#1: Assess your skills: Reflect on your strengths and abilities. Are you a skilled writer, graphic designer, or programmer? Identifying your expertise will guide you to suitable opportunities.

#2: Consider your interests: Pursue a method that excites and motivates you. Passion and dedication are crucial for long-term success. If you love photography, for example, selling stock photos could be an ideal fit.

#3: Time commitment: Determine the amount of time you're willing to invest. Freelancing, for instance, may require more hands-on involvement than affiliate marketing or creating online courses.

#4: Initial investment: Consider the financial investment needed for each method. Some require little to no upfront costs, such as blogging or affiliate marketing, while others might entail expenses, like starting an e-commerce store or investing in rental properties.

#5: Income potential: Research the earning potential of various online methods. Some opportunities, like freelancing or e-commerce, may yield quicker returns, while passive income streams like blogging or online courses may take time to build.

#6: Flexibility: Choose an approach that aligns with your desired work-life balance. If you prefer a flexible schedule, freelancing or content creation might be more suitable than managing an online store.

#7: Long-term prospects: Evaluate the sustainability of your chosen method. Aim for opportunities with long-term growth potential, and avoid those with limited prospects or high market saturation.

#8: Network and learn: Connect with others who have successfully made money online, attend webinars and read industry blogs. Gaining insights from experienced individuals can help you make informed decisions.

#9: Experiment: Don't be afraid to try different methods. Sometimes, the best way to discover the right path is through trial and error. Learn from your experiences and adapt your strategy as needed.

By taking the time to consider these factors, you'll be better equipped to choose an online money-making method that aligns with your skills, passions, and goals.

16 Powerful Ways You Can Make Money with ChatGPT

We'll cover in-depth in Chapters 2, 3 and 4 the top 3 different business ideas to make money with ChatGPT but for now to let you see the potential, here are 16 ways you can make money with ChatGPT:

1. **The Creative Content Factory:** With ChatGPT's writing prowess, you can set up a content creation agency! Offer services like blog writing, social media posts, or copywriting for ads. ChatGPT will be your secret weapon in producing top-notch, engaging content that'll keep your clients coming back for more!
2. **ChatGPT Tutoring & Education:** Use ChatGPT to develop personalized study materials, create educational resources, or even answer questions as a tutor. Help students excel in their studies while you excel in your bank account. Talk about a win-win!
3. **Personal Assistant & Concierge:** Offer an exceptional ChatGPT-based virtual assistant service that takes care of a wide array of tasks for busy professionals, entrepreneurs, or anyone needing an extra hand.
4. **Master of Ceremonies:** Leverage ChatGPT's talent for generating engaging and creative text to become a sought-after event planner. Write captivating speeches, personalized invitations, and create memorable event themes. Host unforgettable events and parties that'll have people talking for months!
5. **ChatGPT eCommerce Guru:** Use ChatGPT to craft irresistible product descriptions and optimize your online store. Create a seamless customer service experience by integrating ChatGPT into your store's chat system, providing

instant and helpful responses. Watch your sales skyrocket as customers rave about their shopping experience!

6. **Niche Expert Ghostwriter:** Use ChatGPT to become a sought-after ghostwriter in a specific niche. Produce ebooks, articles, and guides that showcase your "expertise" and rake in the dough as clients line up to work with you. Say hello to your new bestseller status!

7. **Social Media Manager Extraordinaire:** Employ ChatGPT to create attention-grabbing social media content that boosts engagement and drives traffic. Offer your top-notch social media management services to clients looking to grow their online presence. Watch those likes, shares, and dollars roll in!

8. **The Resume Guru:** Help people land their dream jobs by using ChatGPT to craft stellar resumes and cover letters tailored to each individual's experience and the positions they're applying for. Your expert touch will have your clients singing your praises as they climb the career ladder!

9. **Life Coach:** Use ChatGPT to offer personalized life coaching services, from goal-setting to habit-building. Provide motivation, inspiration, and guidance to help your clients transform their lives. They'll thank you later, and so will your wallet!

10. **Translator & Localization Wizard:** Harness the power of ChatGPT to provide translation and localization services for businesses and individuals alike. Be the bridge between languages and cultures, making the world a smaller, more connected place while you watch your earnings grow!

11. **Character Creation:** Let ChatGPT be your partner in bringing to life unforgettable characters that resonate with your audience. Its AI-driven insights can help develop rich personalities, backgrounds, and motivations.

12. **Copywriting:** Boost your marketing efforts by leveraging ChatGPT's persuasive writing capabilities. Create attention-grabbing headlines, engaging product descriptions, and compelling calls-to-action that convert.
13. **Blogging:** Enhance your blog with fresh, relevant, and engaging content generated by ChatGPT. Keep your audience coming back for more and grow your online presence.
14. **Screenwriting:** Use ChatGPT to create compelling scripts for film, television, and other visual media. Bring your stories to life on the screen with engaging dialogue and well-crafted scenes.
15. **Poetry and Songwriting:** Tap into ChatGPT's creative potential to craft evocative poems and catchy song lyrics. Explore new themes, styles, and structures to create emotionally resonant art.
16. **Ebook Creation:** Harness the power of ChatGPT to create informative and engaging ebooks. You can make more money if you offer valuable content that meets the needs of digital readers today.

As you stand at the precipice of a new chapter in your life, I encourage you to take that leap of faith and embrace the abundant opportunities that await you in the realm of online income generation. Each venture outlined in this guide represents a chance to redefine your career, pursue your passions, and create a life that aligns with your values and aspirations.

Key Takeaways

We learned:

- 3 Stages to Making Money Online
- Explored 16 diverse ways to monetize ChatGPT, from content creation and marketing strategies to AI-driven consultations and beyond.

Now that we have set the foundations of how money works and examples on how to monetize ChatGPT to whet your appetite and give you a taste of the joys of the earning potential. In the next upcoming 3 chapters, we will be diving in-depth on the top 3 business ideas that could be your ticket to financial freedom. I promise it's worth the suspense, so keep reading and let's uncover this treasure together!

Chapter 2
Making Money with Content Creation That You Need To Know

Imagine a world where you can write effortlessly, where captivating content flows seamlessly from your fingertips. This dream can be your reality, in this chapter we will embark on a life-changing journey as you explore the fascinating world of "Using ChatGPT to Start and Grow A Successful & Persuasive Online Blog." This business idea will guide you to unlock the incredible potential of AI-driven content creation and empower you to build a thriving online presence that leaves an indelible impact on your readers.

The world of blogging is vast and full of potential, but finding the perfect niche can be a daunting task. I'm going to help you explore the best methods to effortlessly research profitable niches for blogging. By following the steps outlined below, you will have the tools to identify the most lucrative opportunities within your areas of interest.

How To Effortlessly Research Profitable Niches for Blogging?

1. **Identify Your Interests and Passions:**

The foundation of a successful blog is a genuine passion for the subject matter. Take some time to list your interests, hobbies, and expertise. This will help you narrow down potential niches and ensure you enjoy writing about the topic.

2. Analyze Market Trends and Demand:

Keep your finger on the pulse of the market by analyzing trends and demand for your potential niches. Use tools like Google Trends, Trend Hunter, and Statista to gather information about the popularity of various topics over time. This will help you identify niches with growing interest and high potential.

3. Assess Keyword Search Volume and Competition:

Keyword research is essential to find profitable niches with high search volume and low competition. Tools like Google Keyword Planner, SEMrush, and Ahrefs can provide valuable insights into the number of monthly searches and competition levels for specific keywords related to your niche.

4. Evaluate Monetization Potential:

Monetization is a crucial factor when selecting a profitable niche. Research affiliate programs, advertising revenue, sponsored content opportunities, and the potential for selling your products or services. High-paying affiliate programs and advertising revenue can be a strong indicator of a niche's profitability.

5. Study Successful Blogs in Your Niche:

Examine the top blogs in your potential niches to learn what makes them successful. Analyze their content strategy, posting frequency, and audience engagement. This will give you a better understanding of the best practices and help you identify gaps in the market.

6. **Utilize Social Media and Online Communities:**

Engage in social media platforms and online communities related to your potential niches. Platforms like Reddit, Facebook groups, and Quora can provide valuable insights into your target audience's pain points and preferences, further refining your niche selection.

7. **Test Your Niche:**

Once you've narrowed down your options, create a few blog posts or articles related to your chosen niche. Share them on social media and online communities to gauge audience interest and feedback. This will help you validate your niche before investing significant time and resources into your blog.

By following these seven steps, you can effortlessly research and identify profitable niches for blogging. Remember to stay true to your passions, monitor market trends, analyze keywords, and assess monetization potential. By doing so, you will create a successful blog that provides value to your readers and generates income.

How To Come Up with A Domain Name With ChatGPT?

Before you start creating your own blog, you need to have a domain name, so think of your blog's niche. Are you into travel, fashion, or maybe even tech? Jot down some keywords related to your niche.

Once you have your keywords, ask ChatGPT for domain name suggestions. For example, if you're a foodie, you could ask, "Create a list of different domain name ideas for a food blog". Don't be shy! The more specific your request, the better the suggestions.

Refine and repeat: ChatGPT will whip up some domain names for you, but don't be afraid to ask for more or provide additional information. Maybe you want to focus on vegan recipes or budget travel. Keep refining your request until you get the perfect domain name.

Make it personal: To make your domain name truly memorable, try adding a personal touch. Share some details about yourself with ChatGPT, like your name or a quirky fact, and see what creative suggestions it comes up with.

Test the waters: Once you've got a shortlist of potential domain names, bounce them off your friends and family to see which ones resonate with them. They'll be able to give you honest feedback and help you pick the winner!

How To Brainstorm Keywords & Questions?

Incorporating high volume keywords and addressing popular questions within your content is essential for optimizing your blog posts. While ChatGPT is an excellent tool for idea generation, it is not designed to assess keyword volume. To obtain accurate data, it is advisable to utilize specialized SEO tools.

Free options, such as Google Keyword Planner and Google Search Console, can provide valuable insights into popular search phrases and their respective search volumes. However, for a more comprehensive analysis, consider investing in paid SEO tools like Moz, Ahrefs, or SEM Rush. Though these services typically start at approximately $100 per month, they offer precise data and advanced features that can significantly enhance your content strategy.

#1 Secret Technique:

Leverage ChatGPT to generate keyword ideas, and then verify their search volume and ranking difficulty using your chosen SEO tools. To optimize your content further, experiment with ChatGPT by asking questions like:

"What are some related keywords on the topic of [topic]?"

"What are some blog posts you could write to appeal to users with transactional intent on the topic of [your topic]?"

By combining the idea generation capabilities of ChatGPT with the analytical power of SEO tools, you can create engaging and highly optimized content that effectively targets your desired audience.

#2 Secret Technique:

You can also use the role-playing technique here to generate keywords. Use this prompt:

Prompt: Act like a SEO expert. Generate a list of words you should include on a blog post around green investment. Share only the words separated by a Comma.

Response by ChatGPT: Green investment, sustainable finance, ESG criteria, renewable energy, climate change, carbon footprint, impact investing, socially responsible investing, green bonds, clean technology, etc…

How Can You Brainstorm Frequently Asked Questions with ChatGPT to Know Your Target Audience?

Overcoming writer's block and creating compelling content can be achieved by focusing on answering relevant questions within your articles. By providing detailed information and input to ChatGPT, you can enhance the quality of the output, resulting in a more engaging and informative piece.

Incorporating these questions in your text, particularly as headings, not only aids in structuring your content but also serves as valuable long-tail keywords for SEO. Many search queries are formulated as questions, so addressing them directly increases the likelihood of your content being discovered.

To gather popular questions related to your topic, consider using the following prompt:

"What are some frequently asked questions on [topic]?"

Additionally, utilize resources like Answer the Public to find more questions and consult Google Search Console to identify keywords you already rank for that are pertinent to your topic.

For added SEO benefits, consider generating an FAQ schema by prompting ChatGPT with:

"Generate an FAQ rich snippet schema in JSON-LD."

After identifying potential keywords and questions, validate their search volume using an SEO tool such as Google Keyword Planner, Ahrefs, or another tool of your choice. This verification ensures that you are targeting phrases that users are actively searching for, thus maximizing your content's effectiveness.

How To Find a List of Data & Examples

You can use these prompt formulas to find a list of data & examples.

Prompt Formula 1: As a [topic expert], provide a comprehensive list of scientific evidence and real-life examples that showcase the significance of [topic].

Prompt Formula 2: Assuming the role of a [topic expert], present a selection of data-driven examples and research findings that validate the importance of [topic].

Prompt Formula 3: Pretend you're a [topic expert] and offer a collection of scientifically-supported examples and statistics that demonstrate the relevance of [topic].

Prompt Formula 4: Embody a [topic expert] and share an array of case studies and empirical data that emphasize the critical role of [topic] in our lives.

Prompt Formula 5: As an expert in [topic], supply a series of fact-based examples and research-backed data that underscore the key aspects of [topic].

Prompt Formula 6: Taking on the persona of a [topic expert], furnish a well-curated list of examples and data, substantiated by scientific research, to illustrate the value of [topic].

Prompt Formula 7: Act like a [topic expert]. Share a list of examples and data, backed with science, to support [topic]

By implementing these strategies, you can overcome writer's block and create engaging, SEO-optimized content that caters to the needs and interests of your target audience. Let's dig into brainstorming blog post ideas.

How to Brainstorm Blog Post Ideas?

To use ChatGPT to brainstorm blog post ideas and generate detailed, well-researched content, you can follow these steps:

#1: Define your niche or topic: Start by specifying the niche or topic you want to generate blog post ideas for. This will help ChatGPT provide relevant suggestions. For example, "Generate blog post ideas for a digital marketing blog."

#2: Provide specific criteria: Make your request more detailed by including specific criteria or themes you want to focus on. For example, "Generate blog post ideas for a digital marketing blog, focusing on social media strategies and trends."

#3: Request examples or case studies: To ensure that the content is well-researched, ask ChatGPT to provide examples or case studies within the blog post ideas. For example, "Generate blog post ideas for a digital marketing blog, focusing on social media strategies and trends, and include examples or case studies."

ChatGPT Response:

"10 Successful Social Media Campaigns: A Deep Dive into the Strategies That Worked"

#4: Request content outlines: To further ensure that the content is well-researched and detailed, ask ChatGPT to generate content outlines for the selected blog post ideas. For example, "Create a content outline for a blog post on '10 Successful Social Media Campaigns: A Deep Dive into the Strategies That Worked.'"

#5: Draft the content: Once you have the blog post ideas and outlines, you can use ChatGPT to help you draft the content. For each section of the outline, provide a specific writing prompt. For example, "Write an introduction for a blog post on '10 Successful Social Media Campaigns: A Deep Dive into the Strategies That Worked.'"

If everything's looking good, just tell it to "Proceed to write the next section." Keep using that line until you've got the whole article covered.

Pro-tip: If ChatGPT suddenly stops mid-section without finishing, don't stress. Just type "continue" and it'll pick up where it left off.

Want to have more control over the length of each part? Simply specify the word count, like "Write a 300-word introduction."

#6: Human Editing and Proofreading: So, you've got a "finished" blog post in your hands, but hold up! It's time to flex those human editing muscles and give it some extra love. Trust me, with just 30 minutes of tweaking, you can transform an "okay" and kind of robotic piece into a high-quality, super helpful post. Let's go!

Here's your editing to-do list:

1. Fact-check everything! AI might sound confident, but sometimes it's way off. Don't let that slip through the cracks.

2. Make sure the information is fresh and up-to-date.

3. Spruce up your article's SEO by playing with headings, links, bullet points, blockquotes, and callouts.

4. Oh, and ChatGPT's got your back for link suggestions! Just ask it to "Suggest where to add links in this text. Output the same text, but make the text that could be a link bold."

5. Don't forget to add images and alt text!

6. Chop out anything that's too generic or unhelpful.

7. Last but not least, infuse the post with your unique writing style.

#7 Final Polish: Once you're done editing the blog post, don't forget to clean up any human errors, like spelling, grammar, and sentence structure. Good news: you can use ChatGPT to give your content a final polish!

Just remember to keep the snippets short—stick to 300 words or less at a time, or it might struggle to handle it.

Here are some handy prompts tips:

- Proofread this:
- Fix the spelling & grammar
- Expand or summarize a specific section
- Change the tone, more formal/informal/friendly
- Rewrite this using simpler language
- Add some humor
- Add relevant emojis as bullet points (perfect for social media)

By following these 7 steps, you can effectively use ChatGPT to brainstorm blog post ideas and generate well-researched, detailed content.

Prompt templates:

Using ChatGPT to brainstorm blog post ideas can be an efficient way to generate creative and engaging content. By creating prompt templates, you can quickly come up with numerous ideas for your blog posts. Here are five prompt templates that you can use to generate ideas with the help of ChatGPT:

1. **"Listicle" Template:**

    Generate a list of X [topic-related] tips/ideas/hacks/strategies for [target audience]

Example: "Generate a list of 10 productivity hacks for work-from-home professionals"

2. **"How-to" Template:**

    Explain how to [action] in order to [outcome] in [specific context/industry]

Example: "Explain how to create an effective social media marketing strategy in order to boost brand awareness in the fashion industry"

3. **"Comparison" Template:**

    Compare and contrast [product/service/method A] with [product/service/method B] for [target audience] considering [criteria]

Example: "Compare and contrast using online courses with attending in-person workshops for aspiring writers considering cost, effectiveness, and networking opportunities"

4. **"Interview/Expert" Template:**

   Come up with questions to interview [industry expert] on [topic] to provide valuable insights for [target audience]

Example: "Come up with questions to interview a renowned psychologist on the impact of social media on mental health to provide valuable insights for parents"

5. **"Case Study/Success Story" Template:**

   Outline a case study/success story on how [individual/organization] achieved [outcome] through [strategy/method]

Example: "Outline a case study on how a small business owner increased their online sales by 200% through effective email marketing campaigns"

Simply input these templates into ChatGPT, substituting the relevant keywords, and you'll have a variety of blog post ideas generated for you to choose from.

How To Conduct Research with ChatGPT?

Start by entering a general keyword related to your subject into ChatGPT. For example, if you're crafting a blog post about "digital marketing," type "digital marketing" into ChatGPT.

- ChatGPT will produce a list of ideas that serve as starting points for your research. Pick any idea generated by ChatGPT and use it as a research question or blog post topic.

- Once you have a topic idea, input a related question, and ChatGPT will supply pertinent information for your blog post.
- ChatGPT can also generate related topics to broaden your research. Input a keyword relevant to your subject, and ChatGPT will offer several connected topics to gather more data.
- As you work with ChatGPT to generate ideas and questions for your subject, take notes on the information it provides. This helps organize your research and ensures you have all the necessary details for an insightful blog post.

Using ChatGPT for research guarantees you have all the necessary information for an informative and engaging article.

Example: Let's say you're writing a blog post about "tips for cooking healthy meals at home." You can use ChatGPT to generate ideas and questions related to your subject.

You can start by entering a general keyword related to your subject, such as "healthy cooking."

- ChatGPT will produce several ideas related to healthy cooking, like "healthy meal prep," "healthy snacks," and "healthy meal planning."
- Pick one idea, like "healthy meal prep," and enter a related question, such as "what are some healthy meal prep ideas?"
- ChatGPT will offer relevant information for your blog post, including suggestions like "preparing meals in advance," "using fresh ingredients," and "incorporating lean protein."
- Use ChatGPT to generate related topics for further research. For instance, enter "meal planning," and ChatGPT might

recommend connected subjects like "meal planning apps" or "meal planning for busy schedules."
- Take notes on the information provided by ChatGPT as you generate ideas and questions related to your subject, helping you organize your research and compile all necessary details for an informative blog post.

Using ChatGPT for conducting research, you can create ideas and questions related to your subject, collecting relevant information to craft an informative and engaging blog post.

Preparing ChatGPT

Alright, before we get the ball rolling with ChatGPT, we gotta prep it for what it's gonna do.

We'll toss in some key context, sprinkle in keywords, and give it the lowdown on the writing style we want. And hey, always make sure to say, "Do not start writing the post yet. Please wait for my instructions." Trust me, it keeps ChatGPT from jumping the gun and messing up the process.

First prompt:

I want you to act as a blogger and [topic] expert. You are writing a blog post for your [industry] blog. The topic of the post will be [what the post is about]. This post should be helpful for people [choosing/buying/researching/learning etc...].

It should direct them to [take an action]. There should be a call to action at the end of each section. The length of the blog post will be [number] to [number] words.

The tone will be [informal/ helpful/ persuasive/ professional/ authoritative etc…].

You should be writing as an individual blogger with a personal approach so do not use plural first-person to refer to yourself e.g., "our", "we". Only use singular first-person. Do not use passive voice.

I want you to include these keywords: [keywords][you want][to rank for]

Here is the list of [things if this is a listicle post]: [thing1][thing2]

Do not start writing the post yet. Please wait for my instructions.

Here's another way to prepare ChatGPT To generate specific and valuable content for your readers

Prompt Characteristics	Prompt Specifications	Example 1 of Prompt Specification	Example 2 of Prompt Specification	Example 3 of Prompt Specification
What [is the expected task]	To fill with your task main action	Create 5 title tags	Create a hub and spoke model from a list of these keywords, taking their search intent into consideration to group them: remote work, remote work Spain, remote work USA, remote work Europe, remote work uk, remote work productivity, remote work tips, remote work guides, remote jobs, remote communication, remote companies, remote work trends	Generate 10 article ideas about popular "remote work advice" topics

Where [Is it going to be used]	To fill with the location where your task will be used	to be featured in a white jeans category page	to be used to structure a remote work site resources section	to be used to identify articles opportunities to write about in a remote work website
How [is the format / language / structure / tone / length / characteristics / constraints]	To fill with the characteristics of your task	descriptive, in English, relevant, engaging, following SEO best practices, of no more of 50 characters each	The hub and spoke model should be listed in bullet points, in English, along with the search intent of each of the keyword	The ideas should be listed in bullet points, making each of them unique without repeating already published ones, along with the user search intent that they will fulfill and the sentiment
Who [is the target audience]	To fill with your task audience	potential jeans buyers	professionals looking to work remotely	professionals looking to work remotely

When [is it going to be used]	To fill with your task timing	at an ongoing basis	for a resources section to be published in April 2023	for an article to be published in April 2023
Why [you want to use it, the expected goal]	To fill with your task purpose	to engage the audience and rank better in search results	to attract and fulfill the need of a digital nomad professional audience	to attract and fulfill the need of a digital nomad professional audience

How To Brainstorm the Perfect Blog Post Title?

I like to tackle the little bits first, just to make sure ChatGPT's on the right track. If it's not quite there, you can add more context and give it another shot.

When it comes to prompts, you've got two choices:

- Hit it with a "Write 10 title ideas for this blog post"
- Or, ask for "10 alternative titles for [Your draft blog post title]"

The first one's great for getting those creative juices flowing. The second? Perfect if you've got a draft title and want to see some funky new twists.

This method is a total game-changer for me. Titles used to be my nemesis, but now I can whip up something catchy and keyword-packed in no time.

Write Meta Description

Before diving into the main blog post, you can give ChatGPT a little warm-up exercise.

You can ask it to, "Write a meta description for this article." If it's not quite there yet, no worries! You can toss in more context and info, then give it another shot.

Doing this fine-tuning now means we won't be wasting precious time when we get to the actual post-writing part. Trust me, it's a real time-saver!

Bonus # 1: Write an Entire Blog post with only 2 prompts

Act like a [desired expertise to write the blog post].

Craft a blog post that provides a detailed overview of the features and benefits of your [product/service] tailored to the specific needs and pain points of your [target audience persona].

Use [language and tone] that resonates with your [target audience persona] to demonstrate how your [product/service] addresses their unique [concerns/desires].

Integrate strong SEO words like [share a list generated by ChatGPT].

Include these specific examples/data/testimonials [add them here] to validate your claims and build trust with your audience.

Leverage [the power of storytelling OR use a case study] to illustrate the impact of your [product/service] on [your target audience persona].

End with a [strong and clear/compelling/urgent] call-to-action that encourages your audience to take the [next/required] step towards [purchasing/signing up for/trying] your [product/ service].

As you create your content, keep in mind any [industry-specific nuances/cultural sensitivities] that may impact the effectiveness of your messaging.

It's a blog post about [benefit of your product/service], not an ad for [product/service].

Include the required formatting of an efficient blog post to boost SEO, with an introduction, body, Title tags, Heading tags, and Meta description.

Bonus # 2: Create and Publish 500 Blog Posts In A Day

This Bonus plan is to create 500 AI generated articles in 1 day and publish them. You'll need only 3 tools:

- Google Sheets
- ChatGPT
- Grammarly

STEP #1:

Find 3-5 websites from your niche (competitors), copy-paste your competitors blog titles into Google Sheets. You should have a list of 500 different blog titles. All the different blog titles will be in Column A.

STEP #2:

For this, you will need the "GPT for Sheets and Docs" Plugin,

Simply go into your Google Sheets, Select Extensions > Add-ons > Get Add-ons,

From there, you will be directed to Google Workspace Marketplace, do a search for "GPT for Sheets and Docs" Plugin and install, do note that it only works in Google Chrome.

Once installed, go to Google Sheets, Select Extensions > GPT for Sheets and Docs > Enable GPT functions

STEP #3:

Use ChatGPT to rewrite titles of articles,

Since all the different blog titles are in Column A, Column B will be your New Article Name.

Example:

Row A1= 6 Myths About Selling a Home in January, Debunked by Top Agents

Your New Article Name will be in B1, so input the following formula in B1:

=GPT(A1, "Rewrite Title")

And the new title would be: Debunking the Myths: Selling A Home in January Is Possible!

STEP #4:

Use ChatGPT to create Meta Titles and Meta Descriptions for the New Article Name.

Since Column B is the New Article Name, Column C will be for the Meta Title and Column D will be for the Meta Descriptions.

For Meta Title, input the following formula in C1:

=GPT(B1, "Create Meta Title shorter than 60 characters")

For Meta Description, input the following formula in D1:

=GPT(B1, "Create Meta Description shorter than 160 Character")

Note: For all GPT commands, it must be in quotations and since the meta title and meta description is for the new article name, we will be using B1 instead of A1.

STEP #5:

Use ChatGPT to write an article.

Column E will be the content for your blog, input the following in E1:

=GPT(B1, "Write a blog")

STEP #6:

For this step you'll need Grammarly,

Copy and Paste the text into the backend of your website (I use WordPress) and accept all grammatical suggestions.

STEP #7:

Add the finishing touches, edit some of the text to be in H2/H3 Headings, add internal links if you want, add pictures, copy and paste the Meta Title and Meta Description and you're done.

Simply hit that PUBLISH button and go to step #5 to generate more articles.

Key Takeaways

You have now become a pro for how to:

- Unlock the power of keywords and questions to fuel your content ideas

- Become a research ninja, gathering all the info you need to write top-notch posts

- Prep ChatGPT like a pro, setting the stage for a smooth collaboration

- Craft the ultimate "killer" post title that grabs attention and won't let go

- Whip up a captivating meta description that'll reel in those clicks

- Build a rock-solid blog post outline to guide your writing journey

- Dive into each section, making your outline come to life

- Add the human touch to transform AI-generated content into a masterpiece

- Give your writing a final polish, making it shine like the star it is

Whoa, hold on! You've come this far, so don't stop now! In the next chapter, I'm spilling the beans on a mind-blowing business idea that could send your income soaring to new heights. Trust me, you don't want to miss this!

Chapter 3
Level Up Your Content Marketing With ChatGPT

This chapter is your radioactive spider-bite, unlocking the hidden potential of ChatGPT to turn you into a content marketing superhero. Get ready to save the day and rake in the big bucks with your newfound powers!

I'm going to spill the beans about how ChatGPT for Content Marketing will be a game-changer in your quest to create outstanding content that resonates with your audience and make crazy money in no time. As it's time to bid adieu to mediocrity and usher in a new era of unparalleled content creation with ChatGPT.

10 Easy Steps to Monetize Content Marketing with ChatGPT

Are you ready to turn your passion for content marketing into a money-making venture? I've put together 10 easy steps to guide you through the exciting journey of monetizing your content.

1. **Find your sweet spot:** Choose a specific topic or industry that you're passionate about and have expertise in. Conduct market research to ensure there's sufficient demand and monetization potential. Consider the competition, long-term viability, and opportunities for growth within the niche. Analyze existing content in the niche to identify gaps and opportunities for unique content creation. When selecting your niche, it's essential to strike a balance between your interests, expertise, and the monetization potential to ensure long-term success and sustainability.

2. **Define your target audience:** Understand who your ideal customers are, their preferences, pain points, and how your content can help them. Create detailed audience personas that include demographics, interests, and behavior patterns. By having a clear understanding of your target audience, you can tailor your content to address their specific needs and desires, making it more engaging and effective. Regularly conduct surveys, monitor audience feedback, and analyze data to refine your audience personas and ensure your content remains relevant and valuable to your readers.

3. **Plan it out:** Outline the types of content you'll produce, the platforms you'll use, and a posting schedule. Your content plan should be based on your niche, target audience, and chosen monetization strategies. Experiment with various content formats, such as blog posts, videos, podcasts, and infographics, to determine what resonates best with your audience. Establish a consistent posting schedule to keep your audience engaged and maintain a strong online presence. Regularly review and update your content plan to stay relevant and adapt to evolving audience preferences.

4. **Build your online home:** Create a professional online presence where you can showcase your content and build your audience. Choose a domain name and hosting provider that align with your brand and niche. Design your website with user experience and accessibility in mind, ensuring it's easy to navigate, visually appealing, and mobile-responsive. Use your website or blog as a hub for all your content, providing a centralized location where your audience can easily access and share your work.

5. **Team up with ChatGPT:** Utilize the AI-powered tool to generate high-quality, engaging, and persuasive content that resonates with your audience. ChatGPT can assist with

various content formats, from blog posts and social media updates to email newsletters and video scripts. Collaborate with the AI model to brainstorm content ideas, create outlines, and optimize your content for SEO. By leveraging ChatGPT, you can save time and resources while maintaining a consistent brand voice and messaging across different content types and platforms.

6. **Spread the content:** Share your content on social media, email newsletters, and other relevant channels to reach your target audience. Develop a multi-channel promotion strategy that includes organic and paid methods to maximize your reach and exposure. Collaborate with influencers, guest post on reputable websites, and engage in online communities to expand your network and boost your content's visibility. Monitor the performance of your promotional efforts and adjust your strategy as needed to optimize engagement and conversions.

7. **Optimize for SEO:** Implement search engine optimization strategies to improve your content's visibility on search engines and drive organic traffic. Research and incorporate relevant keywords, optimize meta tags, headings and create high-quality backlinks to boost your search engine rankings. Use ChatGPT to generate SEO-friendly content that effectively integrates targeted keywords without sacrificing readability and user experience. Regularly review and update your SEO strategies to stay current with search engine algorithm changes and maintain your competitive edge.

8. **Grow your email list:** Offer valuable resources like e-books or guides in exchange for your audience's email addresses, allowing you to nurture leads and promote your products or services. Develop an email marketing strategy that includes regular content updates, personalized recommendations, and

exclusive offers to keep subscribers engaged and encourage conversions. Use ChatGPT to craft compelling email content that resonates with your audience and drives action. Monitor your email marketing performance, such as open rates, click-through rates, and conversions, to optimize your strategy and maximize your return on investment.

9. **Choose a monetization strategy:** Based on your niche, audience, and content type, select one or more strategies to generate revenue. Popular monetization options include affiliate marketing, sponsored content, selling digital products or services, subscription-based content, paid webinars, and donations. Assess the viability of each strategy for your specific niche and audience, and choose the ones that align best with your goals and values. Diversify your income streams to minimize risk and maximize your earning potential. As your audience grows and your content evolves, continuously evaluate and adapt your monetization strategies to ensure ongoing success.

10. **Monitor and analyze results:** Keep track of your content's performance and revenue generation to make data-driven decisions for improvement. Utilize analytics tools, such as Google Analytics and social media insights, to track key performance indicators (KPIs) like traffic, engagement and conversions. Regularly review your monetization strategies to identify areas for optimization and growth. Gather feedback from your audience to gain insights into their preferences and expectations and use this information to refine your content and offerings. By consistently monitoring and analyzing your results, you can make informed decisions that drive the success of your content marketing and monetization efforts.

Monetizing content marketing with ChatGPT involves a combination of strategic planning, consistent content creation, effective promotion, and ongoing analysis. By following these ten easy steps, you can build a successful online presence, establish your authority in your niche, and generate sustainable revenue through various monetization strategies.

6 Monetization Strategies for Content Marketing

This section delves into how ChatGPT can be utilized to enhance different monetization strategies, providing insightful content to help readers make money online.

#1: Affiliate Marketing

Affiliate marketing involves promoting other companies' products or services and earning a commission for each sale or lead generated through your marketing efforts. ChatGPT can assist in crafting persuasive and engaging content for your affiliate marketing campaigns.

a. Product Reviews and Comparisons: You can use ChatGPT to create well-researched and comprehensive product reviews or comparisons, highlighting the features and benefits of the products you are promoting. By providing valuable information, you can help potential buyers make informed decisions and increase the likelihood of conversions.

Prompt templates:

1. "Top 5 [Product Category] Reviewed: Which One is the Best Fit for Your Needs?"

2. "[Product A] vs. [Product B]: A Comprehensive Comparison to Help You Decide"

3. "Unboxing and In-Depth Review: [Product Name] - Is It Worth the Investment?"

4. "Our Top Picks: The Best [Product Category] in the Market Today"

5. "Expert Review: Analyzing the Pros and Cons of [Product Name]"

b. Tutorial Content and How-To Guides: ChatGPT can generate step-by-step tutorials and guides related to the products you are promoting. By showcasing practical applications and real-life use cases, you can demonstrate the value of the products and services to your audience, leading to higher conversion rates.

Prompt templates:

1. "Step-by-Step Guide: How to Set Up and Use [Product Name] Like a Pro"

2. "Mastering [Product Category]: Tips and Tricks for Getting the Most Out of Your [Product]"

3. "How to Choose the Perfect [Product Category] for Your Specific Needs"

4. "The Ultimate Guide to [Product Name]: Features, Benefits, and Best Practices"

5. "Getting Started with [Product Category]: A Beginner's Tutorial on [Product Name]"

c. Email Marketing Campaigns: You can leverage ChatGPT to craft engaging email newsletters and promotional content, targeting subscribers with personalized product recommendations and offers. By using persuasive language and compelling calls-to-action, you can boost click-through rates and affiliate sales.

Prompt templates:

1. **Subject:** "Discover the Secret to [Desired Outcome] with [Product Name]"

   Content: Share the benefits of using the product, personal experiences, and a strong call to action with an affiliate link.

2. **Subject:** "Exclusive Offer: Save [X%] on [Product Name] - Limited Time Only!"

   Content: Promote a special deal or discount for the product and encourage subscribers to act quickly with an affiliate link.

3. **Subject:** "Unlock Your Full Potential with [Product Name]: Our Top Recommendations"

   Content: Share a curated list of the top products in the category, highlighting the benefits of each and include affiliate links.

4. **Subject:** "Real Stories: How [Product Name] Changed Lives"

   Content: Share testimonials and success stories from people who have used the product and include an affiliate link for the reader to learn more.

5. **Subject:** "Last Chance: Don't Miss Out on [Product Name]'s Amazing Benefits"

   Content: Remind subscribers of the product's value and the limited-time nature of any offers, including a clear call to action with an affiliate link.

#2: Sponsored Content and Advertisements

Partnering with brands to create sponsored content or host advertisements on your website or blog is another effective monetization strategy. ChatGPT can help you create high-quality content that seamlessly integrates promotional elements while maintaining your audience's interest.

a. Sponsored Blog Posts: Collaborate with ChatGPT to write informative and engaging blog posts that naturally incorporate sponsored products or services. By providing valuable content that resonates with your audience, you can maintain their trust while generating revenue from sponsored collaborations.

Prompt templates:

1. "Exploring the Future of [Industry]: A Partnership with [Sponsor Name]"

2. "How [Sponsor Name]'s Innovative [Product/Service] Is Revolutionizing [Industry/Market]"

3. "Behind the Scenes: An Exclusive Look at [Sponsor Name] and Their Groundbreaking [Product/Service]"

4. "Case Study: How [Sponsor Name] Helped [Customer/Client] Achieve [Desired Outcome]"

5. "Maximizing [Product/Service] Value: Tips and Best Practices from [Sponsor Name]"

b. Ad Copywriting: Utilize ChatGPT to create compelling ad copy for display and native advertisements. By crafting eye-catching headlines and persuasive descriptions, you can increase click-through rates and ad revenue.

Prompt templates:

1. "Introducing [Product/Service]: The Ultimate Solution to [Problem]"

2. "Transform Your [Industry/Market] Experience with [Product/Service] by [Company Name]"

3. "Limited-Time Offer: Get [X%] Off [Product/Service] and Achieve [Desired Outcome] Faster"

4. "Unlock Your Full Potential with [Product/Service] from [Company Name]"

5. "Experience the [Product/Service] Difference: Elevate Your [Industry/Market] Game Today"

c. Sponsored Social Media Content: Leverage ChatGPT to generate creative and share-worthy social media content that features sponsored products or services. By integrating promotional elements into your social media strategy, you can boost brand visibility and generate additional income.

1. "Excited to announce my partnership with [Company Name]! Their incredible [Product/Service] has truly made a difference in my life. #sponsored #ad"

2. "Ready to level up your [Industry/Market] experience? Don't miss [Product/Service] from [Company Name]! #partner #ad"

3. "Exclusive deal alert: Save [X%] on [Product/Service] from [Company Name] for a limited time only! Don't miss out on this opportunity! #sponsored #promo"

4. "I'm loving my new [Product/Service] from [Company Name]! It has helped me achieve [Desired Outcome] in record time. #partner #ad"

5. "Thrilled to collaborate with [Company Name]! Their innovative [Product/Service] is a true game-changer in the [Industry/Market]. #sponsored #ad"

#3: Selling Digital Products and Services

Creating and selling digital products or services, such as eBooks, courses, and webinars, can be a lucrative monetization strategy. ChatGPT can play an instrumental role in the development and promotion of these offerings.

a. Content Creation: you can use ChatGPT to generate well-researched and informative content for eBooks, online courses, and webinars. By providing high-quality and valuable material, you can establish yourself as an expert in your niche and attract paying customers.

Prompt templates:

1. "Unlock Unlimited Potential: Introducing Our [Digital Product/Service] for [Industry/Market] Professionals"

2. "Master [Topic] with Our Comprehensive [Digital Product]: The Ultimate Resource for [Target Audience]"

3. "Achieve [Desired Outcome] Faster with Our Exclusive [Digital Service]: A Comprehensive Solution for [Target Audience]"

4. "Revolutionize Your [Industry/Market] Journey with Our Premium [Digital Product/Service]"

5. "Discover the Secret to [Desired Outcome]: Our [Digital Product/Service] Unveiled"

b. Sales Copy and Landing Pages: Collaborate with ChatGPT to create persuasive sales copy and landing pages for your digital products and services. By highlighting the benefits and value proposition, you can entice potential buyers and increase conversions.

Prompt templates:

1. "Experience the Power of [Digital Product/Service]: Transform Your [Industry/Market] Success Today"

2. "Introducing [Digital Product/Service]: The Ultimate Solution to [Problem] for [Target Audience]"

3. "Maximize Your [Industry/Market] Results with [Digital Product/Service]: Get Started Now"

4. "Unlock the Full Potential of [Digital Product/Service]: Achieve [Desired Outcome] and Elevate Your [Industry/Market] Game"

5. "[Digital Product/Service]: Your One-Stop Solution for [Problem] in the [Industry/Market]"

c. Promotional Content: Leverage ChatGPT to create promotional content for your digital offerings, such as email campaigns, blog posts, and social media updates. By consistently promoting your products and services, you can drive traffic to your sales pages and generate revenue.

Prompt templates:

1. "Limited-Time Offer: Save [X%] on Our Exclusive [Digital Product/Service] and Achieve [Desired Outcome] Faster"

2. "Upgrade Your [Industry/Market] Skills with Our Comprehensive [Digital Product/Service]: Get Started Today"

3. "Don't Miss Out: Exclusive Discounts on Our [Digital Product/Service] for [Industry/Market] Professionals"

4. "Experience the [Digital Product/Service] Difference: Elevate Your [Industry/Market] Performance Today"

5. "Unlock Your Full Potential with Our [Digital Product/Service]: Claim Your Exclusive Offer Now"

#4: Subscription-Based Content and Membership Sites

Offering premium content through subscriptions or membership sites can provide a stable source of recurring revenue. ChatGPT can help you create exclusive content that entices users to subscribe and retain existing members.

a. Premium Content Creation: Use ChatGPT to develop exclusive articles, reports and other content formats reserved for your premium subscribers or members. By offering high-quality, value-driven content, you can justify the subscription fee and maintain a loyal customer base.

Prompt templates:

1. "Unlock Exclusive Access to Our Premium [Industry/Market] Content: Join Our Membership Program Today"

2. "Get Ahead in [Industry/Market]: Discover Our Members-Only In-Depth [Topic] Analysis"

3. "Elevate Your [Industry/Market] Knowledge with Our Premium Content Library: Become a Member Now"

4. "Experience the Power of Premium [Topic] Insights: Join Our Membership Community Today"

5. "Get Unlimited Access to Our Expert [Industry/Market] Content: Sign Up for Our Membership Program"

b. Personalized Content: Leverage ChatGPT to create personalized content tailored to individual subscribers or members, based on their preferences and interests. This level of customization can enhance the user experience, leading to higher retention rates and customer satisfaction.

Prompt templates:

1. "Transform Your [Industry/Market] Journey with Personalized Content Tailored to Your Needs: Join Our Membership Site"

2. "Discover Your Personalized Path to [Desired Outcome]: Become a Member and Unlock Custom [Industry/Market] Content"

3. "Maximize Your [Industry/Market] Success with Custom Content Curated Just for You: Join Our Membership Community"

4. "Get Personalized Recommendations and Expert Guidance on Your [Industry/Market] Goals: Sign Up for Our Membership Program"

5. "Unlock Your Full Potential with Custom Content Designed for Your Unique [Industry/Market] Journey: Become a Member Today"

c. Member-Exclusive Offers and Updates: Collaborate with ChatGPT to craft member-exclusive offers, discounts, and updates, creating a sense of exclusivity and value for your subscribers. By nurturing your relationship with members, you can encourage long-term loyalty and recurring revenue.

Prompt templates:

1. "Exclusive Member Perks: Get Access to Special Offers and Discounts by Joining Our Membership Program"

2. "Stay Ahead of the Curve with Members-Only Updates and Early Access to Our Latest [Industry/Market] Content"

3. "Join Our Membership Community and Enjoy Exclusive Offers on [Industry/Market] Products and Services"

4. "Get the Insider Scoop: Sign Up for Our Membership Program and Receive Exclusive [Industry/Market] Updates and Offers"

5. "Unlock a World of Exclusive Benefits: Become a Member and Enjoy Special Offers, Discounts, and More"

#5: Paid Webinars and Online Workshops

Hosting paid webinars and online workshops is another effective way to monetize your expertise and content. ChatGPT can assist in planning, promoting, and executing these events, ensuring their success.

a. Content Development: Use ChatGPT to develop engaging and informative content for your webinars and workshops, including presentations, scripts, and supplementary materials. By providing valuable insights and actionable advice, you can attract attendees and establish yourself as a thought leader in your industry.

Prompt templates:

1. "Master [Topic] with Our Comprehensive Paid Webinar: A Complete Guide for [Target Audience]"
2. "Unlock the Secrets to [Desired Outcome] with Our Exclusive Online Workshop: Reserve Your Spot Now"
3. "Transform Your [Industry/Market] Skills with Our In-Depth Paid Webinar on [Topic]"
4. "Achieve [Desired Outcome] Faster: Sign Up for Our Premium Online Workshop on [Topic]"
5. "Discover Advanced Strategies in [Topic]: Join Our Intensive Paid Webinar for [Target Audience]"

b. Event Promotion: Leverage ChatGPT to create promotional content for your webinars and workshops, such as email invitations, blog posts, and social media updates. By reaching a wider audience and generating interest, you can increase sign-ups and revenue.

Prompt templates:

1. "Limited Spots Available: Register Now for Our Exclusive [Topic] Webinar and Boost Your [Industry/Market] Skills"

2. "Don't Miss Out: Secure Your Seat for Our Upcoming Online Workshop on [Topic] and Achieve [Desired Outcome]"

3. "Upgrade Your [Industry/Market] Expertise: Register for Our Premium [Topic] Webinar Today"

4. "Exclusive Opportunity: Join Our [Topic] Online Workshop and Unlock Your Full [Industry/Market] Potential"

5. "Last Chance: Book Your Spot in Our [Topic] Paid Webinar and Transform Your [Industry/Market] Performance"

c. Post-Event Follow-Up: Collaborate with ChatGPT to craft post-event follow-up emails and content, thanking attendees for their participation and offering additional resources or upsells. By maintaining communication with attendees, you can foster ongoing relationships and potentially convert them into loyal customers.

Prompt templates:

1. "Thank You for Attending Our [Topic] Webinar: Access the Replay and Additional Resources Now"

2. "Missed Our [Topic] Online Workshop? Get Access to the Recording and Exclusive Bonus Content"

3. "Maximize Your [Topic] Webinar Experience: Download the Presentation Slides and Access Additional Resources"

4. "Continue Your [Industry/Market] Journey: Get Access to the [Topic] Webinar Recording and Exclusive Content"

5. "Stay Ahead in [Industry/Market]: Access the [Topic] Online Workshop Replay and Enhance Your Skills"

#6: Donations and Crowdfunding

For content creators who prefer a more direct approach to monetization, soliciting donations or launching crowdfunding campaigns can be a viable option. ChatGPT can help you create persuasive content that encourages your audience to support your work financially.

a. Donation Request Content: Utilize ChatGPT to craft sincere and compelling donation requests, explaining the value your content provides and how their support can help you continue creating high-quality material. By connecting with your audience on a personal level, you can increase the likelihood of receiving donations.

Prompt templates:

1. "Support Our Mission to [Desired Outcome]: Make a Donation and Help Us Make a Difference"

2. "Every Dollar Counts: Help Us Reach Our Goal and Fund [Project/Initiative]"

3. "Join Our Community of Supporters: Contribute to Our Cause and Make a Lasting Impact"

4. "Together, We Can Achieve [Desired Outcome]: Donate Today and Help Us Create a Better Tomorrow"

5. "Help Us Continue Our Work in [Industry/Market]: Your Generous Donation Makes a Difference"

b. Crowdfunding Campaigns: Leverage ChatGPT to create captivating crowdfunding campaign content, including project descriptions, updates, and promotional materials. By effectively communicating your goals and vision, you can inspire potential backers to contribute to your campaign.

Prompt templates:

1. "Be Part of Our Journey: Support Our [Project/Initiative] Crowdfunding Campaign and Help Us Reach Our Goal"

2. "Join Our Crowdfunding Effort: Contribute to [Project/Initiative] and Make a Lasting Impact in [Industry/Market]"

3. "Help Us Bring [Project/Initiative] to Life: Support Our Crowdfunding Campaign and Become a Part of the Change"

4. "Your Contribution Matters: Join Our Crowdfunding Campaign for [Project/Initiative] and Help Us Make a Difference"

5. "Invest in Our Vision: Support the [Project/Initiative] Crowdfunding Campaign and Help Us Shape the Future of [Industry/Market]"

c. Gratitude and Appreciation Content: Collaborate with ChatGPT to generate personalized thank-you messages and content for your supporters, expressing your gratitude and appreciation for their contributions. By acknowledging their support, you can strengthen your relationship with your audience and foster long-term loyalty.

Prompt templates:

1. "Thank You for Your Generous Support: Together, We Are Making a Difference in [Industry/Market]"

2. "We Couldn't Have Done It Without You: A Special Thank You to Our Donors and Supporters"

3. "Your Contributions Matter: Thank You for Supporting Our [Project/Initiative] and Helping Us Achieve [Desired Outcome]"

4. "Grateful for Our Community: A Heartfelt Thank You to Everyone Who Contributed to Our Cause"

5. "Celebrating Your Support: Thank You for Helping Us Bring [Project/Initiative] to Life"

How to use ChatGPT for Idea Generation For Marketing Campaigns?

A way to use ChatGPT for idea generation is by asking it to brainstorm various marketing angles or campaign themes based on your product or service. Just provide some basic information and let the AI work its magic, coming up with creative suggestions that'll give your marketing efforts a unique twist.

Practical Examples of Instructions That You Can Enter Into ChatGPT To Generate Ideas For Multiple Marketing Purposes

The trick to generating high-quality content with ChatGPT is to give it clear and detailed instructions, or prompts. Just remember to replace generic words like "product" with a specific description of what you're trying to sell. The more precise you are with your prompts, the better. Now, the examples you'll see below are just a few ways to use ChatGPT for creating marketing content, but there's so much more you can do with it! The idea isn't to copy these examples word for word, but to let them inspire you to come up with your own unique ways of using ChatGPT based on your specific needs.

Article Writing:

- "Write a detailed article about the latest trends in AI technology."
- "Write an elaborate opinion article about the impact of social media on people's lives."
- "Write a review of the following [book title, movie, series or video game]."
- "Write a travel guide about Madrid intended for a tourist who has never visited the city."

Content generation for social media:

- "Create an Instagram post that promotes our new product."
- "Write a tweet with its corresponding hashtags about the benefits of traveling by train."
- "Create a Facebook post about our new seasonal promotion."

Email Content generation:

- "Write a commercial email to offer customers a 20% discount on their next order."
- "Write an email to thank customers for their loyalty."
- "Write the subject and body of an email to announce a special private sale."
- "Write an email to invite customers to a special event."
- "Write the body of an email to promote our monthly newsletter on technology trends."

Script generation for promotional videos and animations:

- "Write a script for a promotional video for a new product."
- "Write a detailed script for a 20-second advertisement promoting a sports drink."
- "Write a dialogue between two characters for a science fiction video game."
- "Write a script for the pilot episode of a television series in which the protagonist is an executive who has lost her job."
- "Write a script for an animated series for children in which the main characters are a dog and a cat."

Product description writing:

- "Write a detailed, persuasive description of our new mobile phone model."
- "Write an attractive description for our summer clothing line for men."
- "Write a commercially oriented description highlighting the features of our new coffee maker."

Generation of scripts for corporate videos:

- "Write a script for a video that shows how our company is helping the community."
- "Write a script for a video introducing our services."
- "Write a script for a corporate video that shows the history of our company."

Generation of content for presentations:

- "Write an introduction that captures the audience's attention for a presentation on the latest trends in the real estate market."
- "Write a summary for a presentation on digital marketing strategies in 2023."
- "Write a conclusion for a presentation on innovations in the automotive industry."

Generation of questions for surveys:

- "Write questions for a survey about customer satisfaction with our service."
- "Write questions for a survey aimed at understanding customers' opinions about our brand."
- "Write questions for a survey that wants to know the audiovisual consumption habits of users."
- "Write a survey for Twitter that asks users about satisfaction with our products."

Generation of content for websites:

- "Write a detailed description of our company for the "About us" section of our website."
- "Write a landing page for our current promotion."
- "Write a persuasive text to request the visitor's email address by offering something in return."
- "Write a frequently asked questions page about our services."
- "Write an introduction for the services section of our website."

- "Write a detailed description for the profile of our team on the website."
- "Write a title and description for our privacy policy page."
- "Write the main sections of a website about nutrition and health."

Generation of scripts for podcasts

- "Draft the outline of a podcast about health".
- "How [specific topic] is changing the [X] industry?"
- "Interview with [expert on the topic] about [specific topic]."
- "Analysis of the latest news related to [specific topic]."
- "Discussion about the impact of [recent trend or event] on [specific industry or field]."
- "Tips and tricks for achieving [specific goal] in [specific topic]."
- "Study of [specific topic] from a [specific perspective].

Generating SEO instructions with ChatGPT

It may come as a pleasant surprise that ChatGPT can serve as your personal SEO consultant. Here are some examples of prompts that you can utilize with ChatGPT to enhance the SEO of any text or website:

Generation of meta titles and descriptions:

- "Write a title and meta description for a website about cycling trips and routes".
- "Write a title and meta description for a blog about vegan recipes".
- "Write a title and meta description for a website about personal finance".

Generation of content with specific keywords:

- "Write an article about home security, including the keywords: security, home, alarms, cameras".
- "Write a content about the advantages of a specific product, including the keywords: product, advantages, features".
- "Write a content about adventure travel with a special focus on eco-tourism, including the keywords: adventure, ecotourism, travel".
- "Write an article about 'how to improve strength training performance', including the keywords 'strength training', 'training routine' and 'strength exercises'".
- "Write a technical article about 'how to improve SEO on your website', including the keywords 'SEO', 'search engine optimization', 'search engine positioning', 'website' and 'organic traffic'".
- "Write a detailed guide about 'how to improve Google positioning', including the keywords 'Google positioning', 'local SEO' and 'page optimization'".

Generation of Titles and Descriptions for Websites:

- "Write an attractive title and description for the home page of our website, including the keywords 'economical hotels in [city]' ".
- "Write a title and description for our SEO services page, including the key- words 'search engine optimization'".
- "Write a title and description for our products page, including the keyword 'consumer electronics'.

Generation of Meta Tags for Websites:

- "Write the meta tags for the page of our natural beauty products, including the keywords 'natural cosmetics', 'sustainable beauty' and 'ecological beauty products'".
- "Write the meta tags for the page of our web design services, including the keywords 'web design', 'responsive design' and 'mobile design".

Generation of H1 and H2 Tags for Titles:

- "Write an HTML code for an H1 title and an H2 subtitle for a home page, including the keywords 'economical hotels in [city]'".
- "Write an HTML code for an H1 title and several H2 subtitles for a page on 'how to improve performance in strength training', including the keywords 'strength training', 'training routine' and 'strength exercises'".

Generation of Alt Tags for Images:

- "Write the HTML code for an alt tag of an image of our product [include product description and brand], including the keyword 'multi-function exercise machine'".
- "Write the HTML codes for several alt tags for the images of a product gallery [include product descriptions], including the keyword 'consumer electronics'".

How to Use ChatGPT for Email Marketing?

ChatGPT has the power to revolutionize your email marketing strategy, making it more personalized, engaging, and effective than ever before. Here, we'll explore six key areas where ChatGPT can help you elevate your email campaigns, from crafting irresistible subject lines to optimizing performance with data-driven insights. Let's dive in and unlock the full potential of ChatGPT in your email marketing efforts!

1. Crafting Irresistible Subject Lines:

You can get your subscribers to open your emails by using ChatGPT to create captivating subject lines that pique their curiosity and stand out in their inbox. With attention-grabbing subject lines, you'll have a better chance of getting your emails noticed and opened. Plus, you can test multiple subject lines with A/B testing to identify which ones drive the highest open rates, ensuring you're always using the most effective approach.

Prompt templates:

1. "Generate 10 catchy email subject lines for promoting a new online course on digital marketing."

2. "Create 5 captivating subject lines for a newsletter announcing an exclusive product launch in the fashion industry."

3. "Provide 7 irresistible subject lines for a series of emails about a limited-time offer on a popular travel package."

4. "Craft 6 attention-grabbing subject lines for a weekly newsletter focused on personal finance tips and advice."

5. "Develop 5 engaging subject lines for an email campaign promoting a new fitness app and its features."

2. Personalizing Your Emails:

You can harness the power of ChatGPT to generate personalized content tailored to your subscribers' preferences, interests, and past behavior. By using dynamic content blocks and merge tags, you can address subscribers by their name, recommend products based on their purchase history, or share content relevant to their interests. Personalized emails not only foster a deeper connection with your audience but also lead to higher engagement and conversion rates.

Prompt templates:

1. "As [name] from [company/industry], write an introductory warm sales email to [prospect name] from [prospect industry and company]."

2. "Hey [prospect name], as our valued customer in the [city], we wanted to inform you about our upcoming event."

3. "Write a 100-word follow-up email to [prospect name] who I've just had a call with and is now ready to [action]."

4. "Write a concise, professional, but funny sales email to a prospect who's ghosting me."

5. "In the style of [well-known salesperson whose tone you like], write an email to a recent customer to ask for a referral."

3. Writing Engaging Email Copy:

You can leverage ChatGPT to create compelling email copy that resonates with your audience and encourages them to take action. By maintaining a consistent brand voice and ensuring your messaging aligns with your target audience's preferences and expectations, you'll keep your subscribers interested and eager to learn more. Engaging copy is crucial for driving clicks and conversions in your email campaigns.

Prompt templates:

1. "As [name] from [company/industry], write an engaging email introducing our new project management tool to [prospect name] at [prospect industry and company]."

2. "As [name] representing [company/industry], craft a captivating email promoting a limited-time offer on our online course to [prospect name] from [prospect industry and company]."

3. "As [name] and a member of [company/industry], write an appealing email showcasing the benefits of our eco-friendly products to [prospect name] at [prospect industry and company]."

4. "As [name] in [company/industry], create an enticing email introducing our innovative fitness app and its features to [prospect name] from [prospect industry and company]."

5. "As [name] from [company/industry], compose an engaging email highlighting our new range of software solutions to [prospect name] at [prospect industry and company]."

4. Automating Your Email Campaigns:

You can use ChatGPT to craft a series of automated emails for various scenarios, such as welcome sequences, cart abandonment reminders, or post-purchase follow-ups. Schedule these emails to be sent out automatically based on specific triggers, ensuring timely and relevant communication with your subscribers. Automation helps you stay connected with your audience without the need for manual intervention, saving you time and effort.

Prompt templates:

1. "Create an automated email sequence to welcome new subscribers, starting with an email offering a limited-time 20% discount on our premium subscription."

2. "Design a series of automated promotional emails for our upcoming holiday sale, including an email featuring top-selling products and special deals."

3. "Develop an automated email campaign for our subscribers, including a BOGO email offer focusing on our best-selling items and other exclusive promotions."

4. "Outline an automated email sequence announcing the pre-order availability of our new product, starting with an email highlighting the special bonus for early buyers."

5. "Craft an automated email campaign to celebrate our company's anniversary, beginning with an email offering exclusive deals and discounts for subscribers."

How Can You Use ChatGPT to Personalize A Cold Email?

Research your prospect. For example, your prospect likes Star Trek, so ask ChatGPT to write an email that connects between Star Trek and your offering.

Prompt: write a cold email to a director of customer advocacy at a SaaS company. Connect between Stark Trek and my company - My

Company. My company is a growth-enablement platform that leverages satisfied customers' experiences to help businesses close more deals faster. With my company you can create advocacy programs that incentivize your customers to speak with prospects, easily create customer reviews and case studies, and distribute the content in a smart way. We also track the success of these programs, so you can see the real ROI of your efforts. The email needs to be 75 words max.

The Result:

Dear [Director of Customer Advocacy],

As a fellow Star Trek fan, I couldn't help but notice how your role as Director of Customer Advocacy parallels that of a ship's counselor - ensuring that your crew (customers) are happy and assisting your mission.

At My Company, we share a similar mission to enable growth by leveraging customer satisfaction through advocacy programs that incentivize referrals, reviews, and social media sharing.

Our platform also provides real ROI tracking. Open to go where no customer advocacy program has gone before?

Live long and prosper,
[Name]

Content Strategy for Emails

Cold Email Direct Format Example 1

Direct format: This format is straightforward and to the point, with a clear and concise message. This helps to get the recipient's attention and convey your message quickly and effectively.

Prompt: Write the guide in the outline format including headings, subheadings, and bullet points to highlight key points.

Cold Email Question Format Example 2

Question format: This format includes a question or series of questions related to the recipient's business. This helps to engage the recipient and start a conversation.

Prompt: Write a cold email recommending the recipient try out my new innovative solution using the Question format - include a question or series of questions related to the recipient's business. Make the fields in brackets so I can use mail merge.

I've shared with you just a handful of the countless ways you can put ChatGPT to work for your marketing needs. The secret sauce? Give it super clear and detailed prompts, so it can whip up top-notch content that's perfect for you. And don't forget, let your creative juices flow and think about how you can tweak these examples to suit your unique situation.

Key Takeaways

In this chapter, you have learned:

- Steps to Monetize Content Marketing with ChatGPT

- Monetization Strategies for Content Marketing
- How to Use ChatGPT for Email Marketing
- How to use ChatGPT For Idea Generation For Marketing Campaigns?
- Generating SEO instructions with ChatGPT
- Leveraging ChatGPT for Content Marketing Success

Now that you've unraveled the mysteries of monetizing content marketing with ChatGPT, it's time to shift gears and embark on an even more exhilarating adventure. Are you ready to skyrocket your income through Social Media Marketing with ChatGPT?

The next chapter is an uncharted territory full of excitement, innovation, and profit. So, buckle up, and let's hit the road to social media stardom, where ChatGPT is your trusty co-pilot, navigating you towards a wealth of opportunities.

Chapter 4
How ChatGPT Is Changing the Social Media Marketing Game

Dive into the captivating world of ChatGPT and learn how it's ushering in a new era of social media marketing that you won't want to miss.

Setting up a social media marketing agency can be highly favorable for individuals seeking to earn money online, as it capitalizes on the ever-growing demand for digital marketing services. As businesses increasingly recognize the importance of a strong online presence, they are willing to invest in expert guidance to improve their social media engagement and reach. So, supercharge your marketing efforts, leverage ChatGPT, and start making crazy money.

With over 3.6 billion people worldwide using social media, the potential to reach and engage with your target audience has never been greater. Discover the 10 best ways to harness the power of ChatGPT for social media marketing, unlocking the door to unprecedented growth and revenue.

10 Best Ways to Use ChatGPT For Social Media Marketing

1. Goal-Oriented Campaigns

Creating goal-oriented campaigns is crucial for any social media marketing strategy. With ChatGPT, you can easily define your objectives, such as increasing brand awareness, driving website traffic, or promoting a new product. The AI can then suggest content ideas that align with your goals, allowing you to create tailored campaigns that resonate with your target audience. Here's how ChatGPT can help:

Define clear goals: ChatGPT can assist marketers in establishing clear, measurable goals for their campaigns, such as increasing brand awareness, driving website traffic, generating leads, or boosting sales. Setting well-defined goals enables marketers to create focused campaigns that yield better results.

Generate relevant content ideas: Based on the campaign goals, ChatGPT can suggest content ideas that resonate with the target audience and align with the brand's objectives. This ensures that the marketing efforts effectively address the audience's needs and interests, leading to increased engagement and conversions.

Optimize content for maximum impact: ChatGPT can help marketers optimize their content by providing insights into the best formats, posting times, and platforms for each campaign goal. This ensures that the content reaches its intended audience at the right time and through the most effective channels.

Monitor and analyze campaign performance: By integrating ChatGPT with analytics tools, marketers can track the performance of their goal-oriented campaigns, identifying key performance indicators (KPIs) and areas for improvement. This allows businesses to make data-driven decisions and adjust their strategies to maximize ROI.

Automate marketing efforts: ChatGPT can streamline the marketing process by automating tasks such as content generation, ad copy creation, and even responding to user comments. This frees up time for marketers to focus on other critical aspects of their business, such as building relationships with customers, analyzing data, and refining their strategies.

Prompt Examples:

To run goal-oriented campaigns using ChatGPT, you can use various prompts tailored to your specific objectives. Here are some examples:

Increase Brand Awareness Prompt:

"Generate content ideas for increasing brand awareness of our eco-friendly clothing line on Instagram and Facebook."

Drive Website Traffic Prompt:

"Suggest engaging social media post ideas that encourage users to visit our website and explore our latest blog articles on healthy living."

Generate Leads Prompt:

"Create a compelling social media post that encourages users to sign up for our free webinar on digital marketing strategies for small businesses."

Boost Sales Prompt:

"Write a persuasive social media caption promoting our limited-time offer on our premium skincare products, emphasizing the benefits and discount."

Improve Customer Retention Prompt:

"Provide ideas for a social media campaign that showcases our exceptional customer support and encourages repeat purchases from existing customers."

Promote an Event Prompt:

"Generate engaging social media content to promote our upcoming charity run, highlighting the cause, date, and registration details."

Launch a New Product Prompt:

"Suggest captivating social media post ideas for introducing our innovative smart home security system, emphasizing its unique features and ease of use."

Build an Email List Prompt:

"Create a social media post that invites users to subscribe to our monthly newsletter for exclusive tips, offers, and industry news."

Encourage User-Generated Content Prompt:

"Propose a social media contest idea that motivates our customers to share their experiences with our products, using a specific hashtag and tagging our brand."

Enhance Brand Reputation Prompt:

"Generate content ideas for showcasing our brand's commitment to sustainability and ethical practices on our LinkedIn and Twitter profiles."

By using these prompts or variations of them, you can effectively leverage ChatGPT to create goal-oriented campaigns that drive results and help you achieve your marketing objectives.

2. Create Content Calendars

Developing a content calendar is essential for maintaining a consistent posting schedule. ChatGPT can help you generate ideas for future posts, ensuring you have a steady stream of engaging content for your audience. By using this AI tool, you can plan out weeks or even months in advance, allowing you to focus on other important aspects of your business.

ChatGPT can provide a variety of content ideas based on your brand, niche, and target audience. Having a well-planned content calendar ensures that you have a consistent stream of engaging content to share with your audience, which helps build brand loyalty and drives traffic to your website or online store.

Prompt example: "Generate 30 social media post ideas for our organic food store, focusing on promoting healthy eating habits, new products, and special offers."

Plan ahead: By using ChatGPT to create a content calendar, marketers and business owners can plan their social media marketing efforts weeks or even months in advance. This helps maintain a consistent posting schedule, which is essential for growing your audience and keeping them engaged.

Optimize posting times: ChatGPT can help you determine the best times to post on various social media platforms, based on your target audience's preferences and online behavior. This ensures that your content reaches your audience when they are most likely to engage, leading to increased visibility and higher chances of conversion.

Align content with marketing goals: Creating a content calendar with ChatGPT allows you to align your social media content with your overall marketing goals, such as promoting a new product, driving website traffic, or growing your email list. This ensures that your social media efforts are focused and effective, ultimately driving better results and revenue.

Adapt to trends and current events: A content calendar created with ChatGPT can help you stay up-to-date with trends and current events relevant to your industry. This enables you to create timely and topical content that resonates with your audience, further increasing engagement and driving sales.

Save time and resources: By automating the content planning process with ChatGPT, marketers and business owners can save valuable time and resources. This allows them to focus on other aspects of their business, such as building customer relationships, analyzing data, and refining their marketing strategies.

Prompt examples

1. Generate Monthly Content Ideas Prompt:

"Generate 30 social media post ideas for our fitness center for the month of May, focusing on workout tips, motivational quotes, member success stories, and upcoming events or promotions."

2. Plan Seasonal Campaigns Prompt:

"Create a content calendar for our online clothing store's summer collection launch, including 15 social media post ideas that showcase new products, highlight special offers, and emphasize the benefits of our summer clothing line."

3. Optimize Posting Schedule Prompt:

"Suggest the best times and days to post on Instagram, Facebook, and Twitter for our vegan restaurant, targeting a young and health-conscious audience. Provide 20 engaging post ideas that emphasize our delicious menu options, sustainability initiatives, and customer testimonials."

4. Align Content with Marketing Goals Prompt:

"Our marketing goal for the next quarter is to increase website traffic and grow our email list. Generate a 3-month content calendar for our digital marketing agency's LinkedIn and Twitter profiles, with 40 post ideas that drive users to our website, showcase our expertise, and encourage newsletter sign-ups."

5. Adapt to Industry Trends and Events Prompt:

"Create a content calendar for our tech blog's social media accounts during the upcoming CES (Consumer Electronics Show) week, including 10 post ideas that cover the latest gadgets, industry trends, and key announcements from the event."

3. Generate Captions

Captivating captions can make your social media posts stand out and encourage user engagement. ChatGPT can help you generate creative and catchy captions that align with your brand's voice and messaging. This AI-powered tool can save you time and effort, allowing you to maintain a consistent posting schedule while keeping your content fresh and engaging.

ChatGPT can help you create engaging, persuasive, and captivating captions for your social media content. Effective captions can lead to increased user engagement, improved brand visibility, and higher conversion rates. Here's how ChatGPT can assist in generating captions and driving revenue:

1. **Enhance post engagement:** ChatGPT can generate creative and catchy captions that capture the audience's attention and encourage them to engage with your content. This increased engagement can lead to a larger following, higher reach, and improved brand visibility, ultimately contributing to revenue growth.
2. **Maintain brand voice consistency:** By providing guidelines on your brand's tone and messaging, ChatGPT can generate captions that consistently align with your brand's voice. This helps create a cohesive and recognizable brand identity, fostering trust and loyalty among your audience, which can translate into higher sales.

3. **Highlight key selling points:** ChatGPT can create captions that emphasize your products' or services' unique features and benefits, persuading potential customers to take action. These persuasive captions can lead to increased click-through rates, driving more traffic to your website or online store and boosting sales.
4. **Encourage user-generated content:** ChatGPT can craft captions that inspire your audience to share their experiences with your products or services, using specific hashtags or tagging your brand. This user-generated content can increase your brand's credibility and exposure, leading to higher conversion rates and revenue growth.
5. **Save time and resources:** By automating the caption creation process with ChatGPT, marketers and business owners can save valuable time and resources. This allows them to focus on other aspects of their business, such as building customer relationships, analyzing data, and refining their marketing strategies.

By using ChatGPT to generate captions for social media content, marketers and business owners can improve user engagement, maintain brand consistency, and effectively showcase their products or services, ultimately leading to increased revenue and business growth.

Prompt example:

Promote a Product or Service Prompt:

"Generate 5 captivating captions for our new noise-canceling headphones, focusing on their superior sound quality, comfort, and sleek design."

Prompt Template Examples:

- "Introducing [Product/Service]: How can it transform your [specific problem/need]?"

Example: "Introducing our new AI-powered social media management tool: How can it transform your brand's online presence?"

- "Discover the secret to [desired outcome] with [Product/Service]"

Example: "Discover the secret to flawless skin with our new organic skincare line"

- "[Product/Service]: The game-changer in [industry] you've been waiting for"

Example: "Our innovative meal planning app: The game-changer in healthy eating you've been waiting for"

- "Unlock your [specific potential] with the power of [Product/Service]"

Example: "Unlock your creative potential with the power of our digital art course"

- "Why [Product/Service] is the ultimate solution for [specific problem/need]"

Example: "Why our eco-friendly cleaning service is the ultimate solution for a spotless and sustainable home"

Highlight a Special Offer or Discount Prompt:

"Create 5 persuasive captions for our upcoming 20% off sale on all skincare products, emphasizing the limited-time offer and the benefits of our natural ingredients."

More examples:

- "Limited Time Offer: Save [Discount]% on [Product/Service] - Don't Miss Out!"

Example: "Limited Time Offer: Save 30% on our Premium Subscription - Don't Miss Out!"

- "Celebrate [Event/Holiday] with an Exclusive [Discount]% Off [Product/Service]"

Example: "Celebrate Earth Day with an Exclusive 20% Off Our Sustainable Products Collection"

- "Flash Sale Alert: Enjoy [Discount]% Off [Product/Service] for the Next [Time Period]"

Example: "Flash Sale Alert: Enjoy 50% Off All E-books for the Next 48 Hours"

- "Unlock a [Discount]% Discount on [Product/Service] with Promo Code [CODE]"

Example: "Unlock a 25% Discount on Our Fitness App Membership with Promo Code GETFIT25"

- "Buy [Product/Service] Now and Get [Additional Product/Service] for Free - Limited Offer!"

Example: "Buy Our Online Marketing Course Now and Get a Free Consultation - Limited Offer!"

Inspire and Motivate Prompt:

"Write 5 motivational captions to accompany our fitness center's workout photos, encouraging followers to stay committed to their health and fitness goals."

More examples:

- "Unlock Your True Potential: [Action/Strategy] to Overcome [Challenge] and Achieve [Goal]"

Example: "Unlock Your True Potential: 5 Strategies to Overcome Procrastination and Achieve Your Dreams"

- "The Power of [Positive Trait]: How Embracing [Trait] Can Lead to [Desired Outcome]"

Example: "The Power of Gratitude: How Embracing Gratefulness Can Lead to a Happier, More Fulfilling Life"

- "From [Undesirable Situation] to [Success]: [Number] Steps to Transform Your [Aspect of Life]"

Example: "From Chaos to Clarity: 7 Steps to Transform Your Workspace and Boost Productivity"

- "Breaking Free from [Limiting Belief]: How to Cultivate [Positive Mindset] and Achieve [Goal]"

Example: "Breaking Free from Self-Doubt: How to Cultivate Confidence and Achieve Personal Success"

- "[Inspirational Figure]: [Number] Lessons We Can Learn from Their [Journey/Success Story]"

Example: "Oprah Winfrey: 5 Lessons We Can Learn from Her Inspirational Journey to Success"

Share Educational Content or Tips Prompt:

"Craft 5 engaging captions for our food blog's cooking tutorial posts, showcasing the ease and deliciousness of our healthy recipes."

- "Master [Skill/Topic]: [Number] Essential Tips for [Specific Goal or Improvement]"

Example: "Master Public Speaking: 7 Essential Tips for Confident and Effective Presentations"

- "The Ultimate Guide to [Topic]: Everything You Need to Know to [Achieve Desired Outcome]"

Example: "The Ultimate Guide to SEO: Everything You Need to Know to Improve Your Website's Rankings"

- "[Topic] 101: [Number] Fundamental Concepts to Understand and Apply in Your [Aspect of Life]"

Example: "Investing 101: 5 Fundamental Concepts to Understand and Apply in Your Financial Life"

- "Top [Number] [Topic] Hacks: Quick and Easy Ways to [Improve/Enhance/Achieve] [Desired Outcome]"

Example: "Top 10 Time Management Hacks: Quick and Easy Ways to Improve Your Daily Productivity"

- "Avoid Common [Topic] Mistakes: [Number] Tips for [Better Results/Success]"

Example: "Avoid Common Gardening Mistakes: 6 Tips for a Thriving, Beautiful Garden"

Encourage User-Generated Content Prompt:

"Generate 5 captions that invite our customers to share photos of their home decor using our furniture products, including a specific hashtag and tagging our brand."

- "Share Your [Product/Service] Experience: Post a Photo/Video with #[Hashtag] and Get Featured on Our Page!"

Example: "Share Your Travel Experience: Post a Photo with #WanderlustAdventures and Get Featured on Our Page!"

- "[Product/Service] Success Stories: Tell Us How [Product/Service] Has Made a Difference in Your Life and Inspire Others!"

Example: "Fitness App Success Stories: Tell Us How Our App Has Made a Difference in Your Fitness Journey and Inspire Others!"

- "Join Our [Topic] Challenge: Share Your Progress Using #[Hashtag] and Win Exciting Prizes!"

Example: "Join Our 30-Day Yoga Challenge: Share Your Progress Using #YogaRevolution and Win Exciting Prizes!"

- "We Want to Hear from You: Share Your [Topic/Experience] Tips and Tricks in the Comments for a Chance to Be Featured!"

Example: "We Want to Hear from You: Share Your Best Work-from-Home Tips and Tricks in the Comments for a Chance to Be Featured!"

- "Calling All [Target Audience]: Show Us Your [Skill/Creation] by Tagging Us and Using #[Hashtag] for a Chance to Win [Prize]!"

Example: "Calling All Foodies: Show Us Your Most Creative Dish by Tagging Us and Using #CulinaryGenius for a Chance to Win a Gourmet Gift Basket!"

By using these prompts or variations of them, you can effectively leverage ChatGPT to create engaging and captivating captions for your social media content, improving user engagement, and driving better results.

4. Find Relevant Hashtags

Hashtags are an integral part of social media marketing, as they help increase visibility and reach. With ChatGPT, you can easily find relevant and trending hashtags for your posts. The AI tool can analyze your content and suggest hashtags that will help your posts reach a larger audience, boosting engagement and driving traffic to your website.

You can find relevant hashtags using ChatGPT by providing a clear description of your brand, niche, or the specific theme you want to target. ChatGPT can then generate a list of hashtags related to the given context, helping marketers increase the visibility of your social media content and reach a wider audience. Here's how you can use ChatGPT to find relevant hashtags:

Define your niche or theme: Begin by giving ChatGPT a clear description of your brand, target audience, or the theme you want to focus on for your content. This information will help the AI generate hashtags that are relevant and specific to your needs.

Prompt example: "Generate 10 relevant hashtags for a sustainable fashion brand that focuses on eco-friendly materials and ethical production practices."

Specify the platform: Different social media platforms may have varying hashtag trends and user behavior. You can tailor your prompt to include the specific platform you want to target, ensuring the generated hashtags are suitable for that platform.

Prompt example: "Generate 10 relevant Instagram hashtags for our vegan bakery, focusing on our plant-based desserts and sustainable packaging."

Request hashtag popularity: If you want to target popular hashtags, you can ask ChatGPT to provide hashtags that are currently trending in your niche or industry. This can help you tap into a larger audience and increase content visibility.

Prompt example: "Generate 10 popular and trending hashtags in the digital marketing industry for our social media marketing agency."

Find long-tail hashtags: Long-tail hashtags are more specific and may have a smaller but more targeted audience. You can request ChatGPT to generate long-tail hashtags related to your niche, helping you reach a more engaged audience.

Prompt example: "Generate 10 long-tail hashtags for our travel blog, focusing on solo female travelers and off-the-beaten-path destinations."

By utilizing ChatGPT to find relevant hashtags, you can increase the visibility of your social media content, reach new audiences, and ultimately boost your brand's online presence.

5. Respond to comments

Interacting with your followers is crucial for building brand loyalty and trust. ChatGPT can help you respond to comments and messages in a timely and personalized manner. The AI tool can generate thoughtful replies that address your followers' concerns or questions, helping you maintain an active presence on social media and foster a sense of community.

You can use ChatGPT to respond to comments on your social media posts by providing the AI with the context of the comment and any specific guidelines for responding. ChatGPT can generate appropriate, personalized, and engaging responses that help maintain a positive brand image and foster customer relationships. Here's how you can use ChatGPT to respond to comments:

Provide the comment context: Share the comment you want to respond to with ChatGPT, including any relevant background information about the post, product, or service that the comment refers to.

Prompt example: "A user commented, 'I love your eco-friendly packaging! Are your products also cruelty-free?' Respond to this comment for our vegan skincare brand."

Specify the tone and style: Guide ChatGPT on the desired tone and style of the response, such as friendly, professional, or playful, to ensure the generated response aligns with your brand's voice.

Prompt example: "A user commented, 'What's the best way to apply your facial serum?' Respond to this comment using a friendly and informative tone for our skincare brand."

Address customer concerns or questions: ChatGPT can help address customer questions, concerns, or feedback by generating responses that provide useful information and demonstrate your brand's commitment to customer satisfaction.

Prompt example: "A user commented, 'I received a damaged item in my order. How can I get a replacement?' Respond to this comment on behalf of our online clothing store, offering assistance and guidance."

Encourage further engagement: Use ChatGPT to craft responses that encourage additional engagement from users, such as asking follow-up questions, prompting them to share their experiences, or directing them to relevant resources.

Prompt example: "A user commented, 'I just completed your online course and loved it!' Respond to this comment for our e-learning platform, thanking them and encouraging them to share their favorite takeaway."

By leveraging ChatGPT to respond to comments, you can ensure timely and engaging interactions with your audience, enhancing your brand's reputation and fostering strong customer relationships. This can ultimately lead to increased customer loyalty, positive word-of-mouth, and higher conversion rates.

6. Find Influencers in Your Niche

Partnering with influencers can significantly boost your brand's visibility and credibility. ChatGPT can help you find relevant influencers in your niche by analyzing their social media profiles and engagement rates. This information can then be used to identify potential partnerships that align with your brand's goals and values, resulting in mutually beneficial collaborations.

While ChatGPT cannot directly search for influencers on social media platforms, it can help you brainstorm ideas for finding influencers in your niche by providing strategies and tips that you can implement in your search. Here's how you can use ChatGPT to get suggestions for finding influencers in your niche:

1. **Provide the niche or industry:** Begin by giving ChatGPT a clear description of your niche or industry, specifying any particular topics or subcategories you want to focus on.

Prompt example: "Suggest strategies for finding influencers in the vegan food and lifestyle niche on Instagram."

2. **Specify the platform:** Different social media platforms may have unique features and tools for finding influencers. Mention the specific platform you want to target so that ChatGPT can tailor its suggestions accordingly.

Prompt example: "Provide tips for finding fitness influencers on YouTube, focusing on home workouts and bodyweight exercises."

3. **Request specific search techniques:** Ask ChatGPT to provide specific techniques or methods for finding influencers, such as using certain tools, searching for specific hashtags, or analyzing engagement metrics.

Prompt example: "Suggest techniques for finding travel influencers on TikTok who specialize in budget travel and backpacking."

4. **Seek tips for evaluating influencers:** Request advice from ChatGPT on how to evaluate potential influencers for collaboration, such as looking for their engagement rates, follower demographics, or previous brand partnerships.

Prompt example: "Provide tips for assessing fashion influencers on Instagram to determine if they are a good fit for partnering with our sustainable clothing brand."

By using ChatGPT to generate ideas and strategies for finding influencers in your niche, you can gain valuable insights to aid your search and ultimately discover influencers who can effectively promote your brand, products, or services to their audience.

7. Products Promotion

Promoting your products effectively is crucial for increasing sales and growing your business. ChatGPT can help you create engaging and persuasive content that highlights your products' key features and benefits. By utilizing the AI tool to craft compelling product descriptions and promotional materials, you can ensure your target audience is well-informed and enticed to make a purchase.

Marketers can use ChatGPT to assist in product promotion by generating engaging and persuasive content for various social media platforms, ad campaigns, and other promotional channels. ChatGPT can help create compelling messages that highlight product features, benefits, and unique selling points, ultimately driving interest and sales. Here's how you can use ChatGPT for product promotion:

1. **Social media content:** ChatGPT can generate a variety of social media content ideas that showcase your products and engage your audience, such as promotional posts, educational content, or user-generated content campaigns.

Prompt example: "Generate 10 social media post ideas for promoting our new line of eco-friendly sneakers, highlighting their sustainable materials and comfortable design."

2. **Ad copy:** Craft persuasive ad copy for various platforms, such as Google Ads, Facebook Ads, or Instagram Ads, by

providing ChatGPT with information about your product, target audience, and desired call-to-action.

Prompt example: "Create a compelling Facebook Ad copy for our weight loss supplement, targeting busy professionals looking for a natural and effective solution to help them lose weight."

3. **Influencer partnerships:** ChatGPT can help you create pitches, campaign ideas, or guidelines for potential influencer collaborations, ensuring a consistent and effective message that resonates with their audience.

Prompt example: "Generate a pitch for partnering with fashion influencers on Instagram to promote our new sustainable clothing collection, focusing on the eco-friendly materials and stylish designs."

4. **Email marketing:** Use ChatGPT to create engaging email copy or newsletter content that promotes your products, offers, or discounts, driving subscribers to take action and make a purchase.

Prompt example: "Write an email promoting our upcoming 30% off sale on all skincare products, emphasizing the limited-time offer and the benefits of our natural ingredients."

5. **Blog content:** ChatGPT can help generate ideas for blog articles or guest posts that promote your products in a more in-depth and informative manner, attracting readers who are interested in learning more about your offerings.

Prompt example: "Suggest 5 blog post ideas that showcase the benefits of our smart home security system, focusing on its advanced features, ease of use, and affordability."

8. Write Viral Posts

Creating viral content can be a game-changer for your brand's social media presence. ChatGPT can help you generate ideas and write posts that have the potential to go viral. By analyzing current trends and user interests, the AI tool can suggest content ideas that are likely to resonate with your target audience, increasing the chances of your posts gaining traction and exposure.

You can use ChatGPT to write viral posts by providing the AI with specific guidelines, such as the target audience, platform, and topic, and requesting ideas or drafts that have the potential to go viral. ChatGPT can help create content that resonates with the audience and triggers an emotional response, increasing the likelihood of shares and engagement. Here's how you can use ChatGPT to write viral posts:

1. **Define your target audience:** Clearly outline your target audience to help ChatGPT generate content that appeals to their preferences, interests, and emotions.

Prompt example: "Generate a viral post idea for our fitness blog's Instagram account, targeting young adults who are interested in bodyweight exercises and healthy living."

2. **Choose the platform:** Different social media platforms have unique content formats, user behavior, and trending topics. Specify the platform you want to target so that ChatGPT can tailor the content accordingly.

Prompt example: "Create a viral tweet idea for our travel agency, focusing on budget travel and adventure experiences."

3. **Identify the emotional trigger:** Viral content often evokes a strong emotional response, such as humor, inspiration, or awe. Guide ChatGPT to generate content that triggers a specific emotion to increase the chances of virality.

Prompt example: "Write an inspiring Facebook post for our non-profit organization that highlights the impact of our recent clean water project, aiming to motivate people to support our cause."

4. **Incorporate trending topics or formats:** Leverage current trends, popular formats, or timely events to make your content more relatable and shareable. Ask ChatGPT to include these elements in your viral post.

Prompt example: "Suggest a viral TikTok video idea for our vegan bakery, incorporating a popular baking trend and showcasing our delicious plant-based desserts."

5. **Request multiple ideas or drafts:** Increase your chances of creating viral content by asking ChatGPT to generate multiple ideas or drafts, allowing you to choose the most promising one or refine the content further.

Prompt example: "Generate 5 viral LinkedIn post ideas for our digital marketing agency, focusing on success stories, industry insights, and valuable tips for businesses."

9. Generate Multi-lingual Captions

Reaching a global audience requires content that is accessible and understandable to users from various backgrounds. ChatGPT can help you generate multilingual captions for your social media posts, allowing you to engage with a diverse audience. This feature is especially valuable for businesses looking to expand into international markets or cater to a multicultural clientele.

You can use ChatGPT to generate multilingual captions for your social media content by providing the AI with the original caption or content and requesting translations in the desired languages. This can help you reach a more diverse audience and expand your brand's global presence. Here's how you can use ChatGPT to generate multi-lingual captions:

1. **Provide the original caption:** Share the original caption or content you want to translate with ChatGPT, ensuring it is clear, concise, and accurately conveys your intended message.

Prompt example: "Translate the following caption for our eco-friendly clothing brand's Instagram post: 'Introducing our new sustainable denim collection, made from recycled materials and designed for comfort and style.'"

2. **Specify the target languages:** Clearly state the languages you want the caption translated into, and if needed, provide any cultural context or preferences specific to the target audience.

Prompt example: "Translate the caption into Spanish, French, and German, keeping the tone friendly and emphasizing the eco-friendly aspects of the collection."

3. **Request multiple translations:** To ensure you have the most accurate and culturally appropriate translations, you can ask ChatGPT to generate multiple versions of the translated captions. This allows you to choose the best option or refine the translations further.

Prompt example: "Provide two translations of the caption into Japanese and Korean, focusing on the stylish design and sustainable materials of the denim collection."

4. **Proofread and refine:** While ChatGPT can generate translations in multiple languages, it is important to proofread and refine the generated translations to ensure accuracy and cultural appropriateness. You may want to collaborate with a native speaker or use additional translation tools to verify the translations.

10. Social Media Ads Copy

Effective ad copy is essential for driving conversions and boosting your return on investment. ChatGPT can help you create persuasive and engaging ad copy for your social media campaigns. By analyzing your target audience and campaign objectives, the AI tool can generate tailored ad copy that appeals to your potential customers and encourages them to take action. This can lead to increased click-through rates, conversions, and overall campaign performance.

You can use ChatGPT to write social media ad copy by providing the AI with essential information about the product or service, target audience, platform, and desired call-to-action. ChatGPT can help create persuasive and engaging ad copy that captures the audience's attention and drives conversions. Here's how you can use ChatGPT to write social media ad copy:

1. **Define your product or service:** Clearly describe the product or service you want to promote, highlighting its unique features, benefits, and selling points.

Prompt example: "We are promoting our online language learning app, which offers personalized lessons, gamified learning, and native-speaking tutors."

2. **Identify your target audience:** Specify your target audience, including their demographics, interests, and preferences, to help ChatGPT tailor the ad copy to resonate with them.

Prompt example: "Our target audience is young professionals aged 25-35 who are interested in learning new languages for personal development and career advancement."

3. **Choose the platform:** Mention the social media platform where you plan to run the ad, as different platforms have unique ad formats, user behavior, and content preferences.

Prompt example: "We want to create an ad copy for a Facebook campaign promoting our language learning app."

4. **Provide the desired call-to-action:** Include the desired call-to-action for your ad, such as signing up for a free trial, downloading the app, or purchasing a subscription.

Prompt example: "The call-to-action for the ad should be to start a 7-day free trial of our language learning app."

5. **Craft the prompt:** Combine the information you've gathered into a comprehensive prompt for ChatGPT, asking it to generate a persuasive ad copy based on the provided details.

Prompt example: "Create a persuasive Facebook ad copy for our online language learning app, targeting young professionals aged 25-35 who are interested in learning new languages for personal development and career advancement. The ad should highlight personalized lessons, gamified learning, and native-speaking tutors, and encourage users to start a 7-day free trial."

Scaling Your Social Media Marketing Agency with ChatGPT

These are the best ways to leverage ChatGPT for various business ideas:

- **E-commerce:** Use ChatGPT to create compelling product descriptions, manage social media accounts, and develop engaging content for email marketing campaigns.
- **Restaurants:** ChatGPT can craft unique social media posts highlighting daily specials, events, or menu items, while also assisting with online reservations and customer inquiries.

- **Real estate:** Employ ChatGPT to develop property listings, create engaging articles on housing trends, and manage social media accounts to attract potential buyers.
- **Fitness and wellness:** ChatGPT can generate personalized workout plans, nutritional advice, and motivational content for social media platforms to help clients reach their goals.
- **Professional services:** Law firms, accounting agencies, and consulting firms can use ChatGPT to share valuable insights, industry updates, and thought leadership content on social media.

Content Generation for Social Media with ChatGPT

Here are some practical examples of prompts for ChatGPT that could be used with the goal of generating unlimited content for social media:

Generation of posts for Facebook:

- "Write a Facebook post announcing a special promotion in our hotels".
- "Write a Facebook post with tips to improve performance in strength training".
- "Write a Facebook post to promote our new line of organic beauty products".
- "Write a Facebook post that announces a new online course on artificial intelligence and makes it appealing to the public. Include a call to action".
- "Write a Facebook post that promotes an upcoming event and generates great excitement in the target audience".
- "Write a Facebook post that shares testimonials and reviews from satisfied customers".

Generation of tweets for Twitter:

- "Write a tweet to announce a 24-hour special promotion in our online store".
- "Write a tweet with some practical tips to improve the SEO of your blog".
- "Write a tweet to share an interesting news related to our industry".
- "Write a tweet with an inspiring or motivational quote related to our industry".
- "Write a tweet that announces a giveaway and generates interaction with the public".

Generation of content for YouTube:

- "Write an optimized description for the YouTube algorithm for a video tutorial on how to use our mobile app".
- "Write a script for a corporate video that shows how our company is helping society".
- "Write an optimized description for a video that promotes a product or service".
- "Write a script for a 10-minute video that shows the practical benefits of using our products."
- "Write a description for a video that shows how to prepare a vegetarian dish using our organic ingredients."
- "Write a script for a video that presents our work team and generates confidence in the public."

Generation of posts for Instagram:

- "Write an attractive description for an Instagram post that will be a photo of our new summer clothing collection".

- "Write an Instagram post to promote a special event that encourages the audience".
- "Write an attractive and curiosity-generating description for an Instagram post that is a photo of [tourist place] from [city]."
- "Write an Instagram post that generates a desire to purchase the product seen in the photo".
- "Write an Instagram post with several images and captions that tells a story related to our brand".
- Keep in mind that it is important to specify the objective of each post and the type of audience it is directed to in order to generate more targeted content.

Key Takeaways

As we wrap up the chapter, here are some key takeaways to remember:

- Embrace the power of ChatGPT to generate high-quality, engaging content at scale.
- Unravel the secrets of using ChatGPT to create persuasive ad copy and improve targeting. By doing so, you'll witness a significant boost in your return on investment (ROI) and make every ad dollar count.
- Delve into the fascinating world of AI-powered chatbots and virtual assistants to learn how ChatGPT can revolutionize customer support and foster long-lasting relationships, ensuring customer satisfaction and loyalty.
- Discover the hidden potential of ChatGPT in extracting valuable insights from data, enabling you to make data-driven decisions that keep you ahead of the competition and set your business apart.

- Explore how ChatGPT can help you automate various marketing tasks, freeing up your time to focus on strategy, growth, and innovation.

As you continue on this exciting journey, the next chapter, "Make Money with Freelancing Using ChatGPT," will reveal even more opportunities for you to capitalize ChatGPT. You'll learn how to harness ChatGPT's capabilities to create a thriving freelancing career, generate additional income, and achieve financial success. So don't wait! Dive into the next chapter and unlock your full potential to make more money with ChatGPT.

Chapter 5
How to Supercharge Productivity As A Freelancer

Prepare to be amazed as we uncover the game-changing potential of ChatGPT for boosting your productivity and helping you dominate the freelance market.

In recent years, the world of freelancing has been revolutionized by the integration of artificial intelligence (AI) tools, and ChatGPT is no exception. This cutting-edge language model has proven to be a game-changer for freelancers, empowering them to deliver high-quality work more efficiently than ever before. In this chapter, we will explore the power of ChatGPT in the freelancing arena and identify the types of projects that are particularly well-suited for this versatile AI tool.

One of the key benefits of using ChatGPT in your freelance work is its ability to adapt to a wide range of topics and industries. No matter your niche or area of expertise, ChatGPT can provide invaluable assistance, helping you to create engaging and persuasive content that meets the needs of your clients. Furthermore, with its impressive language capabilities, ChatGPT can assist you in breaking down language barriers, opening the door to new markets and clients from around the world.

Types of Freelancing Projects Suited for ChatGPT

ChatGPT's versatility makes it an ideal tool for various freelancing projects. These are some of the most common project types that can benefit from ChatGPT's assistance:

1. **Content creation and editing:** ChatGPT can help you draft and edit blog posts, articles, and other written content with ease. Its ability to generate relevant and engaging text makes

it an indispensable tool for freelancers who specialize in content creation.
2. **Social media management:** ChatGPT can assist you in crafting compelling social media posts and managing your clients' social media presence. By utilizing its ability to generate creative captions and responses, you can elevate the quality of your social media management services.
3. **Virtual assistance:** As a virtual assistant, you can rely on ChatGPT to help you draft professional emails, create detailed reports, and manage other day-to-day tasks, saving you time and ensuring top-notch work.
4. **Customer support and chatbots:** ChatGPT's advanced language processing capabilities make it an ideal tool for crafting responses to customer inquiries and developing chatbots that can handle a variety of customer support tasks.
5. **Language translation and localization:** With its multilingual capabilities, ChatGPT can help freelancers offer translation and localization services, enabling you to expand your client base and tap into new markets.

By harnessing the power of ChatGPT in your freelancing endeavors, you can increase your productivity, improve the quality of your work, and ultimately elevate your career. In the following sections, we will delve into the specifics of how to make the most of ChatGPT in your freelance business, ensuring you reap the full benefits of this groundbreaking technology.

Setting Up Your ChatGPT Freelancing Toolkit

To maximize the benefits of ChatGPT in your freelancing career, it's essential to set up a robust toolkit that combines the right ChatGPT plan with other indispensable tools and resources. In this section, we will discuss how to choose the appropriate ChatGPT plan, explore the essential tools and integrations that will boost your efficiency, and guide you through building an impressive freelance portfolio.

Choosing the Right ChatGPT Plan

Selecting the right ChatGPT plan is crucial for ensuring that you have access to the features and resources you need as a freelancer. OpenAI offers various subscription plans, each with its own set of benefits and limitations. When choosing a plan, consider the following factors:

- **Volume of work:** Assess the amount of work you expect to complete with ChatGPT's assistance. If you plan to use it extensively, a higher-tier plan with more generous usage limits may be more suitable.
- **Response time:** Some plans offer faster response times, which can be advantageous for time-sensitive projects or when you need to produce content quickly.
- **API access:** If you're a developer or plan to create custom applications that leverage ChatGPT, ensure that the plan you choose includes API access.

Take the time to compare the different plans available and select the one that best aligns with your freelancing needs and budget.

Essential Tools and Integrations for Success

In addition to choosing the right ChatGPT plan, it's crucial to have a set of tools and integrations that complement ChatGPT and streamline your freelancing workflow. Here are some essential tools to consider:

- **Project management tools:** Utilize platforms like Trello, Asana, or ClickUp to manage your projects, keep track of deadlines, and collaborate with clients.
- **Writing and editing tools:** Enhance your writing with tools like Grammarly or Hemingway, which can help you spot errors and improve your content's readability.

- **Time tracking tools:** Use time tracking software like Toggl or Time Doctor to monitor your work hours, ensuring accurate billing and time management.
- **Communication tools:** Choose a reliable communication platform like Slack or Microsoft Teams for seamless collaboration with clients and team members.

When selecting tools, look for those that offer integrations with ChatGPT, as this will further enhance your efficiency and productivity.

Building Your Freelance Portfolio

A well-crafted freelance portfolio is essential for showcasing your skills and attracting potential clients. Here's how to build an impressive portfolio with the help of ChatGPT:

- **Create diverse samples:** Use ChatGPT to generate a range of content samples, such as blog posts, articles, social media captions, and email templates. This will demonstrate your versatility and expertise in various writing styles and industries.
- **Showcase your best work:** Include high-quality samples that reflect your skills and proficiency with ChatGPT. Don't be afraid to take credit for the work you've done in collaboration with the AI tool, as it demonstrates your ability to harness technology effectively.
- **Organize your portfolio:** Categorize your samples by industry, content type, or other relevant criteria, making it easy for potential clients to find the work that interests them.
- **Include client testimonials:** If you have completed projects with satisfied clients, ask for testimonials that highlight your skills and the benefits of using ChatGPT in your work. This will provide social proof and further enhance your credibility.

By setting up a comprehensive ChatGPT freelancing toolkit, you'll be well-equipped to tackle a variety of projects and maximize your earnings as a freelancer. In the next sections, we will explore how to develop in-demand skills, market your services, and streamline your workflow using ChatGPT.

Developing In-Demand ChatGPT Skills

To thrive in the competitive freelancing market, it's crucial to develop in-demand skills that leverage ChatGPT's capabilities. By honing these skills, you can offer valuable services to clients and set yourself apart from other freelancers. In this section, we will explore the key skills you should focus on and provide examples and templates to help you get started.

Content Creation and Editing

Mastering content creation and editing with ChatGPT allows you to produce engaging, high-quality content that meets your clients' needs. Here are some tips for honing this skill:

- **Learn to customize prompts:** Create effective prompts that guide ChatGPT in generating relevant content. For example, if you need to write a blog post about "The Benefits of Remote Work," your prompt could be: "Write an informative and engaging blog post discussing the top 5 benefits of remote work."
- **Develop your editing skills:** Although ChatGPT can produce impressive content, it's essential to review and edit the text to ensure it aligns with your client's requirements and voice. Familiarize yourself with common editing techniques to polish the AI-generated content.

Social Media Management

ChatGPT can be a powerful ally in managing social media accounts, helping you create captivating posts and respond to user comments. To excel in this area, focus on the following:

- **Craft compelling captions:** Use ChatGPT to generate creative captions for social media posts. For example, prompt it with: "Create an engaging Instagram caption for a post promoting a new fitness app."
- **Monitor and respond to comments:** Train ChatGPT to assist you in monitoring user comments and crafting personalized, on-brand responses.

Virtual Assistance

As a virtual assistant, you can harness ChatGPT's capabilities to handle various tasks efficiently. To develop this skill, consider these tips:

- **Draft professional emails:** Use ChatGPT to generate well-structured emails. For example, prompt it with: "Write a follow-up email to a client requesting feedback on a recent project."
- **Create detailed reports:** Leverage ChatGPT to help you draft comprehensive reports by providing it with relevant data and a clear prompt.

Customer Support and Chatbots

ChatGPT's advanced language processing abilities make it an excellent tool for crafting responses to customer inquiries and developing chatbots. Here's how to develop this skill:

- **Train ChatGPT on support queries:** Feed ChatGPT examples of common customer support queries and responses to help it learn how to handle these inquiries effectively.

- **Build chatbot scripts:** Use ChatGPT to create conversational scripts for chatbots by providing it with conversation examples and desired outcomes.

Language Translation and Localization

With its multilingual capabilities, ChatGPT can assist you in offering translation and localization services. To excel in this area, focus on these tips:

- **Refine your translation prompts:** Provide clear prompts to guide ChatGPT in translating text accurately. For example: "Translate the following English paragraph into French: 'The benefits of remote work are numerous, including increased flexibility and reduced commuting costs.'"
- **Localize content effectively:** Leverage ChatGPT's cultural and linguistic knowledge to adapt content for specific regions or audiences.

By developing these in-demand ChatGPT skills, you'll be well-equipped to offer valuable services to clients and set yourself apart in the freelancing market. In the following sections, we will discuss how to market your ChatGPT freelancing services, streamline your workflow, and expand your business.

Marketing Your ChatGPT Freelancing Services

To attract clients and grow your ChatGPT freelancing business, effective marketing is crucial. In this section, we will explore various strategies for marketing your services, from creating a compelling freelance profile to leveraging social media, networking, and more.

Creating an Effective Freelance Profile

A strong freelance profile is essential for showcasing your skills and attracting potential clients. Follow these tips to create an impressive profile:

- **Highlight your ChatGPT expertise:** Emphasize your experience with ChatGPT and the value it brings to your services. Mention specific projects where you've successfully used ChatGPT to deliver outstanding results.
- **Showcase your portfolio:** Include samples of your ChatGPT-generated work in your profile, demonstrating your ability to produce high-quality content across various formats and industries.

Include client testimonials: Feature positive feedback from clients who have benefited from your ChatGPT-assisted services, providing social proof of your expertise.

Promoting Your Services on Social Media

Social media platforms offer an excellent opportunity to reach a broad audience and promote your ChatGPT freelancing services. Here's how to leverage social media effectively:

- **Share valuable content:** Regularly post informative and engaging content that demonstrates your expertise and highlights the benefits of using ChatGPT in your work.
- **Engage with your audience:** Respond to comments and messages promptly, fostering relationships with potential clients and showcasing your customer service skills.
- **Use targeted hashtags:** Research and use relevant hashtags to increase the visibility of your posts and reach potential clients interested in ChatGPT services.

Networking and Building Relationships

Building relationships with other professionals and potential clients is vital for growing your ChatGPT freelancing business. Consider these networking strategies:

- **Attend industry events:** Participate in conferences, meetups, and webinars related to freelancing, AI, or your

specific niche to connect with like-minded professionals and potential clients.
- **Join online communities:** Engage in forums, LinkedIn groups, and other online communities where freelancers and clients discuss industry trends and share opportunities.

Leveraging Freelance Marketplaces

Freelance marketplaces like Upwork, Fiverr, and Freelancer can help you connect with clients actively seeking ChatGPT services. To make the most of these platforms:

- **Optimize your profile:** Ensure your profile highlights your ChatGPT expertise, features a strong portfolio, and includes client testimonials.
- **Bid on relevant projects:** Regularly search for projects that require ChatGPT skills, and submit tailored proposals that emphasize the value you can deliver.
- **Maintain a high rating:** Provide exceptional service to earn positive reviews and maintain a high rating, increasing your visibility and credibility on the platform.

Crafting Winning Proposals

A well-crafted proposal can make all the difference in winning a client's business. Follow these tips to create persuasive proposals:

- **Address the client's needs:** Demonstrate a thorough understanding of the project requirements and explain how your ChatGPT expertise can help fulfill those needs.
- **Showcase your value proposition:** Highlight the benefits of using ChatGPT in your services, such as faster turnaround times, increased creativity, and cost savings.
- **Provide relevant examples:** Include samples of your ChatGPT-assisted work that are similar to the project at hand, showcasing your ability to deliver the desired results.

By effectively marketing your ChatGPT freelancing services through these strategies, you can attract more clients, increase your income, and establish a successful freelancing career. In the next sections, we will discuss how to streamline your workflow, expand your business, and address legal and financial considerations for ChatGPT freelancers.

Streamlining Your Freelance Workflow with ChatGPT

A well-organized and efficient workflow is essential for maximizing productivity and ensuring consistent, high-quality results in your ChatGPT freelancing business. In this section, we will discuss how to streamline your freelance workflow by effectively managing client communication, organizing projects, and delivering top-notch work with the help of ChatGPT.

Managing Client Communication

Clear and timely communication is crucial for building strong relationships with clients and delivering projects that meet their expectations. Here's how ChatGPT can assist you in managing client communication:

- **Automate email responses:** Use ChatGPT to generate personalized, professional email templates for common scenarios, such as initial inquiries, project updates, and follow-ups. This will save time and ensure consistent communication.
- **Respond to queries efficiently:** Leverage ChatGPT's capabilities to quickly generate accurate, informative responses to client questions or concerns, demonstrating your expertise and commitment to customer service.

Time Management and Project Organization

Effective time management and project organization are vital for staying on top of deadlines and balancing multiple client projects. Here's how to optimize your workflow with ChatGPT:

- **Prioritize tasks:** Use ChatGPT to create a list of daily, weekly, and monthly tasks, prioritizing them based on deadlines, complexity, and client preferences.
- **Automate project updates:** Employ ChatGPT to draft project status reports, keeping clients informed about progress and any potential issues.
- **Integrate with project management tools:** Take advantage of ChatGPT integrations with popular project management tools like Trello and Asana to streamline your task management and ensure seamless collaboration with clients.

Delivering High-Quality Work Efficiently

To succeed as a ChatGPT freelancer, it's crucial to consistently deliver top-notch work while managing your time efficiently. Here are some strategies to help you achieve this balance:

- **Optimize your prompts:** Improve the quality and relevance of ChatGPT-generated content by refining your prompts, specifying the desired tone, format, and context.
- **Edit and review efficiently:** Use ChatGPT to assist in the editing process by generating alternative phrasings or restructuring sentences, helping you polish your work more quickly.
- **Learn from feedback:** Incorporate client feedback and preferences into your prompts and editing process, continuously improving the quality of your ChatGPT-assisted work.

By streamlining your freelance workflow with ChatGPT, you'll be able to manage client communication effectively, stay organized, and deliver exceptional work, ultimately enhancing your reputation and growing your freelancing business. In the following sections, we will explore strategies for expanding your ChatGPT freelancing services, as well as addressing legal and financial considerations for a successful career.

Expanding Your ChatGPT Freelance Business

As your ChatGPT freelancing career progresses, it's essential to explore opportunities for growth and expansion. In this section, we will discuss strategies for identifying growth opportunities, scaling your services and income, and building a team to handle increased demand.

Identifying Opportunities for Growth

To expand your ChatGPT freelance business, it's crucial to stay aware of emerging trends and opportunities in the market. Consider these approaches for identifying growth potential:

- **Monitor industry trends:** Stay up-to-date with the latest developments in AI, freelancing, and your niche industry to spot new applications for ChatGPT and related services.
- **Solicit client feedback:** Regularly ask clients for feedback on your services and inquire about any additional needs or requirements they may have. This can help you identify opportunities to expand your offerings.
- **Explore adjacent niches:** Investigate related industries or niches that could benefit from your ChatGPT expertise, opening up new markets for your services.

Scaling Your Services and Income

As you identify growth opportunities, it's essential to scale your services and income accordingly. Here are some strategies for scaling your ChatGPT freelance business:

- **Develop new offerings:** Leverage ChatGPT's capabilities to create new, in-demand services such as content localization, chatbot development, or virtual assistance.
- **Offer tiered pricing:** Implement a tiered pricing structure that allows clients to choose from different levels of service, such as basic, premium, and enterprise options.
- **Upsell and cross-sell:** Take advantage of opportunities to upsell additional services or cross-sell related offerings to existing clients, increasing your income potential.

Building a Team to Handle Increased Demand

As your ChatGPT freelancing business expands, you may need to build a team to help manage the increased workload. Consider these tips for building a successful team:

- **Delegate tasks strategically:** Identify tasks that can be delegated to team members, such as content editing, client communication, or project management, allowing you to focus on higher-level strategy and business development.
- **Train your team in ChatGPT:** Ensure that all team members are proficient in using ChatGPT, providing them with the necessary training and resources to deliver consistent, high-quality work.
- **Foster a collaborative environment:** Encourage open communication and collaboration among your team, leveraging tools like Slack or Microsoft Teams to facilitate seamless teamwork and knowledge sharing.

By expanding your ChatGPT freelance business through identifying growth opportunities, scaling your services and income, and building a capable team, you'll be well-positioned for continued success in the competitive freelancing market. In the next sections, we will discuss the legal and financial considerations for ChatGPT freelancers, ensuring a solid foundation for your growing business.

Legal and Financial Considerations for ChatGPT Freelancers

As a ChatGPT freelancer, it's essential to be aware of the legal and financial aspects of your business to ensure long-term success and stability. In this section, we will discuss intellectual property rights, setting up your freelance business legally, and managing finances and taxes.

Understanding Intellectual Property Rights

Navigating intellectual property rights when using ChatGPT in your freelance work is crucial to avoid potential legal issues. Consider the following guidelines:

- **Review ChatGPT's terms of service:** Familiarize yourself with the terms and conditions related to content generated by ChatGPT, ensuring you understand the limitations and usage rights associated with the platform.
- **Clarify ownership with clients:** Clearly outline the ownership and usage rights of ChatGPT-generated content in your contracts or agreements with clients, reducing the risk of misunderstandings and disputes.
- **Respect third-party rights:** Ensure that any content generated by ChatGPT does not infringe on the intellectual property rights of others, including copyrights, **trademarks, and patents.**

Setting Up Your Freelance Business Legally

Establishing your ChatGPT freelance business on a solid legal foundation is vital for protecting your interests and ensuring compliance with relevant regulations. Here are some steps to consider:

- **Choose a legal structure:** Determine the most appropriate legal structure for your business, such as a sole proprietorship, partnership, or limited liability company (LLC), based on factors like liability protection, tax implications, and administrative requirements.
- **Register your business:** Register your business with the appropriate government agencies, obtaining any necessary licenses or permits.
- **Draft contracts and agreements:** Create clear, comprehensive contracts and agreements for your clients, outlining the scope of work, payment terms, and intellectual property rights related to ChatGPT-generated content.

Managing Finances and Taxes

Effective financial management and tax planning are crucial for maintaining a profitable ChatGPT freelancing business. Consider these tips for managing your finances and taxes:

- **Separate personal and business finances:** Open a dedicated business bank account and credit card to keep your personal and business finances separate, simplifying accounting and tax preparation.
- **Track income and expenses:** Maintain accurate records of all income and expenses related to your ChatGPT freelancing work, using tools like QuickBooks or FreshBooks to help streamline the process.
- **Plan for taxes:** Understand your tax obligations as a freelancer, including self-employment tax, income tax, and any relevant state or local taxes. Set aside a portion of your income to cover these obligations and avoid financial surprises.
- **Consult a professional:** Consider hiring a certified public accountant (CPA) or financial advisor to help you navigate

the financial and tax aspects of your ChatGPT freelancing business, ensuring compliance and maximizing deductions.

By addressing these legal and financial considerations, you'll establish a solid foundation for your ChatGPT freelancing business, allowing you to focus on delivering exceptional services to clients and growing your income. With the strategies and insights provided in this book, you are now well-equipped to make hundreds of dollars with ChatGPT and enjoy a successful, rewarding freelancing career.

The Future of Freelancing with ChatGPT

The future of freelancing with ChatGPT presents numerous opportunities for growth and innovation. As AI technology becomes increasingly sophisticated, freelancers will be able to leverage ChatGPT for a broader range of tasks, generating higher-quality content and offering more advanced services. This, in turn, will enable freelancers to take on more significant projects, tap into new markets, and ultimately increase their income potential.

In conclusion, the future of freelancing with ChatGPT holds immense potential for those who embrace the opportunities and challenges it presents. By leveraging the strategies and insights provided in this book, you'll be well-equipped to adapt to the changing landscape, stay ahead of the competition, and thrive in the exciting world of AI-assisted freelancing.

As you embark on your ChatGPT freelancing journey, remember that your success lies in your ability to adapt, learn, and grow with the evolving technology. Stay curious, be open to new opportunities, and always strive for excellence in your work. With determination, persistence, and the powerful tool of ChatGPT at your disposal, there's no limit to what you can achieve.

Chapter 6
ChatGPT and Its Alternatives

Step into the fascinating realm of ChatGPT and its alternatives, where creative minds and powerful AI join forces to redefine digital communication.

With its remarkable ability to generate human-like responses and create coherent scripts, ChatGPT has garnered significant attention from users and developers alike. However, as with any groundbreaking technology, there are limitations and challenges that drive the exploration of alternatives.

As the demand for ChatGPT alternatives rises, numerous AI-driven chat applications have surfaced, offering cutting-edge features and unique benefits. In this chapter, we will examine the Top 8 AI content generation tools that can help you craft compelling scripts with just a single click. In this chapter, we delve into the world of ChatGPT and its alternatives, offering a comprehensive guide to help you make informed decisions and unleash the potential of AI-powered chatbot solutions.

8 Best ChatGPT Alternatives in 2023 (Free and Paid)

1. Microsoft's Bing: ChatGPT Alternative by Microsoft

Microsoft's Bing is an innovative and intelligent chatbot solution that leverages the power of OpenAI's ChatGPT and Microsoft's Bing search engine to create a dynamic user experience. By integrating ChatGPT's advanced language understanding capabilities with the extensive information repository of Bing, this chatbot is designed to deliver accurate, contextually relevant, and engaging responses to user queries.

Who created Microsoft's Bing?

Google isn't alone in its pursuit of the AI market. Microsoft, with plans to invest a staggering $10 billion in OpenAI—the company responsible for ChatGPT—has now unveiled its revamped Bing AI search engine. An advanced version of ChatGPT, known initially as the "Prometheus model" but later identified as GPT-4 powers this improved search engine. Microsoft asserts that this new model is swifter and more precise than ever.

Bing's latest iteration also includes a chat mode that incorporates web queries, enabling users to request context-based information. In a recent event, Microsoft showcased this feature by having a user inquire about TV recommendations and then utilize Bing to refine the list. Similar to ChatGPT, Bing can now help users plan trips, discover recipes, seek advice, and much more. Although currently in limited preview, Bing will be entirely free upon its release. Initially accessible through a waitlist, this impressive ChatGPT alternative is now open to stable users.

Services offered by Microsoft's Bing

Microsoft's Bing, as an integration of ChatGPT's language understanding capabilities with Microsoft's Bing search engine, offers a variety of services aimed at enhancing user experience, communication, and information retrieval. Some of the key services provided by Microsoft's Bing include:

- **Intelligent Search Assistance:** Bing ChatGPT can understand and process natural language queries, providing accurate and relevant search results tailored to users' needs. This improves the overall search experience and helps users find the information they're looking for more efficiently.
- **Conversational AI:** Bing ChatGPT can engage users in more interactive and human-like conversations, making it an ideal solution for customer support, virtual assistance, and other applications where seamless communication is crucial.

- **Content Generation:** Leveraging ChatGPT's text generation capabilities, Microsoft's Bing can produce high-quality, contextually relevant content for various purposes, such as blog posts, social media updates, and more.
- **Multilingual Support:** Microsoft's Bing can understand and generate content in multiple languages, making it a versatile tool for global communication and content creation.
- **Knowledge Extraction:** By tapping into the vast information repository of Bing's search engine, Microsoft's Bing can extract and present valuable insights, facts, and data to users in response to their queries.
- **Personalized Recommendations:** Based on users' search history and preferences, Microsoft's Bing can offer personalized recommendations, such as articles, products, or services, that cater to individual interests and needs.
- **Sentiment Analysis:** Microsoft's Bing can analyze the sentiment of user inputs, allowing businesses to gain insights into customer opinions and emotions, which can be useful for market research and customer relationship management.

These services make Microsoft's Bing a versatile and powerful tool for various applications across industries, including customer support, content creation, market research, virtual assistance, and more.

By combining the strengths of ChatGPT and Bing, this solution provides a comprehensive, intelligent, and engaging chatbot experience that can transform the way users communicate and access information in the digital world.

Price Plans

Microsoft's Bing offers various price plans to accommodate the diverse needs and budgets of users. While a free version with limited access to features and API calls may be available, premium plans provide additional benefits, such as higher usage limits, faster response times, and priority support. Detailed pricing information can be found on the official Microsoft's Bing website or by contacting the sales team directly.

Main features of Bing AI

- Bing empowers users to pose in-depth questions of up to 1,000 words, with AI-driven responses to illuminate their understanding.
- Boasting the ability to decipher intricate inquiries, Bing excels at rapidly retrieving pertinent information.
- In cases where ChatGPT-enhanced Bing cannot directly address a query, it thoughtfully curated a collection of relevant results to guide users towards their desired knowledge.

ChatGPT vs. Microsoft's Bing

Harnessing a ChatGPT-inspired AI, Microsoft has pioneered a distinct method to maximize OpenAI's potential, known as the Prometheus model. This innovative approach yields highly precise, current, and customized outcomes, while bolstering security measures. By leveraging OpenAI's prowess to its utmost capacity, the Prometheus model epitomizes the future of artificial intelligence integration.

2. Google Bard

Google Bard is an innovative AI-driven content generation tool designed to create high-quality, engaging, and contextually relevant text for various purposes. This cutting-edge solution leverages the advanced natural language processing and understanding capabilities of Google's AI technology to transform the way users create and interact with written content.

Who created Google Bard?

Google, a leader in technology and AI, developed Google Bard as a result of its dedication to advancing the state-of-the-art in natural language processing and generation. With its extensive expertise in AI and machine learning, Google has crafted a powerful and reliable content generation tool that caters to the needs of writers, marketers, and businesses across various industries.

What Services are offered by Google Bard?

Google Bard, as an AI-driven content generation tool, offers a variety of services aimed at enhancing the content creation process and addressing the needs of writers, marketers, and businesses across various industries. Some of the key services provided by Google Bard include:

- **Content Creation:** Google Bard can generate high-quality, engaging, and contextually relevant content for various purposes, such as blog posts, articles, social media updates, and more, making it an invaluable tool for content creators and marketers.
- **Copywriting Assistance:** Google Bard can be used to create persuasive and compelling copy for advertising, product descriptions, email campaigns, and other marketing materials, helping businesses effectively convey their message and reach their target audience.
- **Creative Writing:** Google Bard can assist with creative writing projects, such as storytelling, scriptwriting, and poetry, by providing suggestions, ideas, or even generating entire sections of text, enabling users to overcome writer's block and explore new creative avenues.
- **Multilingual Content Generation:** With support for multiple languages, Google Bard can generate content in various languages, making it a versatile solution for global communication and content creation.

- **Text Summarization:** Google Bard can analyze and summarize lengthy documents or articles, extracting key points and presenting them in a concise, easy-to-understand format, saving users time and effort.
- **Sentiment Analysis:** By analyzing the sentiment of user inputs or existing content, Google Bard can provide insights into customer opinions and emotions, which can be useful for market research, content optimization, and customer relationship management.
- **Content Optimization:** Google Bard can help users optimize their content for search engines by providing suggestions for keywords, phrases, and structure, ensuring that the content is more likely to rank higher in search results and reach a wider audience.
- **Personalized Recommendations:** Based on users' interests, preferences, and browsing history, Google Bard can offer personalized content recommendations, enhancing the user experience and engagement.

These services make Google Bard a comprehensive and powerful content generation tool that caters to the diverse needs of users and businesses across industries. By harnessing the power of Google's advanced AI technology, Google Bard has the potential to transform the way we create, consume, and interact with written content in the digital era.

Price Plans

Google Bard offers a range of pricing plans designed to accommodate users with different needs and budgets. A free version with basic features and limited usage may be available for those seeking to test the service or use it occasionally. Premium plans, on the other hand, provide additional benefits such as increased usage limits, advanced features, faster response times, and priority customer support. Detailed pricing information can be obtained from the official Google Bard website or by contacting the sales team directly.

Bard Ai's main features

- Google heralds Bard's ability to skillfully craft text and engage in insightful dialogue, elevating the conversational AI experience.
- Bard transcends temporal constraints, offering an expansive, ever-evolving knowledge base that defies chronological boundaries.
- As a pioneering project in Google's AI repertoire, Bard excels at distilling extensive texts into succinct, meaningful summaries.

ChatGPT vs. Google Bard

For individuals seeking the benefits of an AI-powered chatbot, both ChatGPT and Bard warrant thorough exploration. Bard distinguishes itself through its affiliation with the esteemed technology titan, Google.

Owing to Google's vast financial and technological resources, Bard is granted access to avant-garde language models and state-of-the-art innovations, resulting in unparalleled accuracy and data-driven insights. Whether your pursuit involves dependable customer service or rigorous analytics, Bard emerges as a compelling contender in the realm of AI chatbots.

3. ChatSonic

Chatsonic by Writesonic offers an all-encompassing solution to your conversational AI needs. Fueled by GPT-4 and GPT-4 plus (with 32k context), Chatsonic overcomes ChatGPT's limitations by delivering real-time data, image, and voice searches, alongside numerous content creation capabilities. Ranking as the "Best alternative to ChatGPT" worldwide since its launch, Chatsonic has garnered significant attention.

Writesonic also introduces Botsonic, a groundbreaking no-code platform for creating and deploying your personalized ChatGPT AI chatbot. This accessible chatbot builder enables you to effortlessly design a conversational AI experience specifically catered to your website visitors. Enhance your online presence with Botsonic's seamless integration.

Opera, the distinguished search engine, flawlessly incorporates Chatsonic into its browser, enabling over 120 million users worldwide to generate long-form articles, blogs, and other high-quality text effortlessly alongside searches, enriching their browsing experience.

Chatsonic combines the knowledge of a sage, the conversational skills of a therapist, the humor of a comedian, a data scientist's problem-solving expertise, and a novelist's creativity. Furthermore, it never tires, forgets conversations, or creates awkward silence. The potential of Chatsonic is limitless.

Explore Chatsonic's key features:

Factual content creation, including real-time topics

Chatsonic partners with Google search to deliver hyper-relevant content, keeping you informed without switching tabs. Chatsonic is an advanced version of ChatGPT that extracts real-time information from Google.

1. **Persona mode**

Choose from 13 personas to customize your AI chat experience, staying informed or practicing conversations with various AI avatars.

2. Mesmerizing image generation

Utilize two different models, stable diffusion and DALL-E, to create custom images with a refined AI algorithm.

3. Voice response functionality

Chatsonic understands voice commands and reads back responses, providing an interactive conversational experience and saving time.

4. Conversation recall

Chatsonic mimics real-life conversations, recognizing your tone and remembering past interactions for more engaging dialogues.

5. Edit, share, and download conversations

Access, modify, or download your chats for future reference or sharing.

6. Chatsonic API

Effortlessly integrate Chatsonic with your existing software for a seamless user experience, adding robust customer service and communication capabilities to your online platforms. Generate revenue by building multiple apps using the Chatsonic API.

Chatsonic App: A ChatGPT-like experience on your smartphone

Writesonic has recently launched a dedicated mobile application for Chatsonic. At present, the Chatsonic App is available for Android users through the Play Store, with plans to release it for iOS users in the near future.

The Chatsonic app is reminiscent of ChatGPT in terms of ease of use and compatibility with all of Chatsonic's features. On days when opening your laptop isn't an option, but you still have a significant amount of work to complete, the Chatsonic app serves as a valuable resource.

Is Chatsonic a more suitable ChatGPT alternative compared to Bing?

For those seeking a swift and effective content creation tool that also provides current search results, Chatsonic emerges as the prime choice. By leveraging the strengths of both ChatGPT and Google, Chatsonic offers users an extensive collection of over a hundred templates (available on Writesonic) to select from. Instead of waiting for months to access Bing, opt for Chatsonic today and begin crafting remarkable content!

4. YouChat: ChatGPT Alternative for Research

YouChat is an innovative AI-powered messaging platform designed to facilitate seamless, engaging, and contextually relevant conversations between users and their contacts. By leveraging advanced natural language processing and understanding capabilities, YouChat aims to redefine the way people communicate, making it an ideal tool for personal, professional, and group interactions.

Who created YouChat?

YouChat, a brainchild of You.com, emerged from the collaborative efforts of ex-Salesforce professionals in late 2021. This innovative search engine harnesses the power of artificial intelligence to provide users with increasingly refined results, adapting to individual interests and usage patterns over time. While prioritizing user privacy, You.com currently operates without advertisements, delivering a seamless and tailored experience for its users.

Services offered by YouChat

You.com is a search engine that has been flirting with AI chatbots even before Microsoft's Bing. You.com unveiled YouChat in December 2022, and a team of ex-Salesforce experts later upgraded it to YouChat 2.0 in February 2023.

YouChat's unique appeal lies in its Large Language Model (LLM) called Conversation, Apps, and Links (C-A-L), which boasts the ability to blend You.com apps for platforms like Reddit and YouTube into the chatbot's replies.

My experience with YouChat reveals potential, though the app integration remains a work in progress. This approach is reminiscent of "multimodal" chat, where chatbots accept more than just text-based inputs, generate outputs beyond text, or employ a combination thereof. To clarify, while the widely accessible free research preview of ChatGPT is not multimodal, its latest GPT-4 LLM is a multimodal chat model, as it processes image inputs.

For now, Microsoft's Bing remains my top recommendation, as it offers contextual insights akin to YouChat and can produce visuals using the Bing Image Generator. However, for those seeking alternatives to Bing or Bard, YouChat is a noteworthy contender worth considering.

YouChat features that can better serve than ChatGPT:

- YouChat offers insights into common questions, yet occasionally falters as it refines its knowledge base.
- While aspiring to present cutting-edge information, YouChat occasionally experiences lapses, highlighting its ongoing development.

5. Jasper AI: ChatGPT Alternative for writing

Jasper has been a prominent player in the AI content generation sphere for a while and has garnered a positive reception from users. In addition to its content generation capabilities and other services, Jasper has introduced a relatively new chatbot called Jasper Chat. This ChatGPT alternative is built on GPT-3.5 and other language models, partnering with OpenAI. However, unlike ChatGPT, which is versatile enough for anyone, Jasper Chat is specifically tailored for businesses in advertising, marketing, and related fields.

Having said that, anyone looking for an AI chatbot akin to ChatGPT can easily use Jasper Chat. According to the company, Jasper Chat has been trained on billions of articles and various pieces of information in 29 languages up until mid-2021. Although it might not contain the most current information, it can still engage in moderately complex conversations. A handy toggle feature allows users to integrate Google search data, enhancing its capabilities.

During my experience with Jasper Chat, it served as an engaging chat companion, adept at solving riddles, composing video scripts, sharing jokes, and reciting tongue twisters. It also performed well when tasked with creating ad copy. Jasper Chat possesses contextual memory, allowing it to recall previous prompts. However, the company has explicitly stated that it is not a research engine and users should verify the outputs.

Price Plans

Jasper Chat is free, but accessing all features requires subscribing to Jasper's Boss or Business plan. The Boss Plan starts at $49 per month, granting you access to all of Jasper's services. While not the most affordable option, you can try the 5-day trial to determine if it suits your needs.

Jasper Chat's key highlights:

Comprehensive knowledge base up until Summer 2021: Jasper boasts an extensive database, having been trained on a wealth of content from 2021 and earlier. This enables it to provide insightful information on topics from that timeframe.

Intuitive, ChatGPT-inspired interface: The user-friendly interface allows seamless interaction with the AI, making the chatting experience enjoyable and effortless.

Sustained, contextual conversations: Jasper Chat possesses the ability to recall previous discussions, adding depth and context to ongoing chats and fostering a more engaging and continuous conversation.

ChatGPT vs. Jasper Chat

In contrast to Chatsonic, Jasper Chat does not offer certain features such as providing real-time, accurate information, the option to choose different personas, voice command functionality, digital art generation, or API access. For a better understanding of which platform suits your needs, review a comprehensive comparison between Writesonic and Jarvis.

6. Perplexity AI: ChatGPT Alternative for research

Perplexity AI is an alternative to ChatGPT that utilizes OpenAI's API, resulting in effective and engaging responses. With a minimalist design, the website is user-friendly and offers functionalities similar to ChatGPT, such as holding conversations and providing a range of responses. A unique feature of Perplexity is its ability to cite sources for the information it provides, though this can also potentially expose the AI to unintentional plagiarism.

When answering questions, Perplexity cites sources at the end of each sentence, much like Wikipedia, and uses those sources to derive its responses. During the testing period, no evidence of direct copy-pasting was found, which indicates that Perplexity is cautious about its content generation.

The chatbot performed well in various conversations without getting confused. However, it lacks the ability to remember previous prompts for multi-turn responses. Additionally, interaction with the AI is limited to text, so features like voice interaction and persona selection are not available. On the upside, the website offers a convenient dark mode.

Price Plans

The best part about Perplexity AI is that it's entirely free to use and doesn't require an account. You can chat with this ChatGPT-like tool and even explore some of its cited sources. Give it a try and see for yourself.

ChatGPT vs. Perplexity AI

Perplexity is a recently introduced, free ChatGPT alternative in the conversational AI arena. It provides ChatGPT-like functionality, including engaging conversational responses and content generation. Large language models (OpenAI API) power Perplexity AI, which also gathers data from well-known websites like Wikipedia, LinkedIn, and Amazon. However, since it's still in beta, it may sometimes reproduce information verbatim, which can result in plagiarized content.

Here are the main features of Perplexity AI:

- generates concise conversational responses similar to ChatGPT.
- collects information from sources like Wikipedia and cites them.
- offers a straightforward interface without an abundance of complex features.

Perplexity AI Pricing:

Currently, Perplexity is free to use, as it is still in its beta phase. While Perplexity AI can answer a wide variety of questions, it may sometimes display information exactly as it appears in the source, which could involve plagiarism. If you're looking for a ChatGPT alternative that generates unique content and responses, consider trying Chatsonic instead.

7. Rytr: ChatGPT Alternative for writing

This ChatGPT alternative is an AI specifically designed to assist with writing. With the help of a sophisticated language AI model, this ingenious AI writing companion assists copywriters all over the world in content generation for ideation or direct use.

With over 40 use cases and 20 voice tones to choose from, Rytr tailors' content to your specific needs. If English isn't your preference, the AI supports 30+ languages, covering all popular options. Rytr prides itself on producing content that requires minimal editing, aiming for perfection straight out of the box. Additional features include an SEO analyzer, WordPress plugins, and a Chrome extension for expanded functionality.

To begin using Rytr, create an account and then customize settings such as language, tone, use case, creativity, variations, and the central idea. Rytr's versatility extends to a wide range of use cases, from storytelling and business ideas to blog writing, interview questions, and more.

The AI-generated copy is precise and adapts the article's structure based on the selected use case. Rytr offers new users 10,000 characters as part of its free plan, with the option to upgrade for additional benefits via a premium subscription. With a reasonable starting price of $29 per month, Rytr is worth exploring to see if it meets your copywriting needs.

Rytr Pricing Plans: Pros and Cons

Rytr is a powerful AI-driven writing assistant designed to help copywriters and content creators generate well-crafted content for a wide range of scenarios. Powered by an advanced language AI model, Rytr offers an efficient solution for various writing tasks, ensuring accuracy and creativity in your copy.

Price Plans

Rytr offers a flexible pricing structure to cater to different user needs.

- **Free Plan:** New users can access 10,000 characters at no cost, allowing them to test the service and explore its features.
- **Premium Plan:** For a more comprehensive experience, users can upgrade to the premium plan starting at $29 per month, unlocking additional benefits and features.

Pros

- **Versatility:** With 40+ use cases, 20+ tones, and 30+ language support, Rytr is adaptable to various writing requirements.
- **Time-saving:** Rytr generates content quickly, allowing users to save time on ideation and content creation.
- **Minimal editing:** The AI-generated copy typically requires little to no editing, streamlining the content creation process.
- **Enhanced functionality:** Rytr includes an SEO analyzer, WordPress plugins, and a Chrome extension, offering added value for users.
- **Customization:** Users can personalize language, tone, creativity, and other settings to ensure the generated content matches their preferences.

Cons

- **Limited free plan:** The 10,000-character limit on the free plan may not be sufficient for users with extensive writing needs.
- **Subscription cost:** Although the premium plan is reasonably priced at $29 per month, it may not be affordable for everyone.
- **Dependence on AI:** While Rytr is efficient and accurate, it may still lack the human touch and nuanced understanding that a professional writer can provide.

Rytr is an innovative AI-powered writing assistant that offers a flexible, customizable, and efficient solution for various writing tasks.

ChatGPT vs. Rytr

RYTR and ChatGPT are AI-powered language models that leverage deep learning techniques for text generation. This comparison article delves into their features, capabilities, and distinctions, including AI technology, output quality, editor, workflow management, supported languages, plagiarism checker, SEO, community, character limits, mobile-friendliness, a free trial, and a monthly price. By understanding these differences, users can determine which technology best meets their needs and requirements.

RYTR, developed by Canadian AI company Element AI, is designed to generate text in specific styles or tones, making it suitable for applications like content creation and customer service. In contrast, ChatGPT, a larger and more advanced language model from OpenAI, has been trained on diverse internet text and can perform various language tasks, such as text completion, translation, summarization, and question answering.

While ChatGPT is considered one of the most advanced language models available, RYTR's specialized training may give it an edge in generating text with a specific style or tone. The choice between RYTR and ChatGPT ultimately depends on the particular requirements of a given task.

Feature comparison between RYTR and OpenAI's GPT-3 (ChatGPT):

- **AI Technology:** Both RYTR and GPT-3 employ deep learning techniques for text generation, but their specific techniques and algorithms may vary.
- **Output Quality:** RYTR excels in generating text with specific styles or tones, while GPT-3 is highly capable across a range of language tasks.
- **Editor:** RYTR's editor availability is unclear, and OpenAI's GPT-3 API does not include one.
- **Workflow Management:** Information on RYTR's workflow management is scarce, and the GPT-3 API does not provide workflow management tools.
- **Supported Languages:** RYTR's supported languages are unclear, while GPT-3 supports numerous languages, including English, Spanish, French, German, Chinese, and more.
- **Plagiarism Checker:** It's uncertain whether RYTR offers a plagiarism checker, and the GPT-3 API does not include one.
- **SEO:** SEO capabilities for RYTR are unclear, and the GPT-3 API does not provide SEO tools.
- **Community:** RYTR's community size and activity are unknown, while OpenAI boasts a large, active community of developers and researchers working with GPT-3.
- **Character Limits:** RYTR's character limits are unclear, and GPT-3 API character limits may vary depending on the use case and pricing plan.
- **Mobile-Friendly:** RYTR's mobile-friendliness is uncertain, while the GPT-3 API can be accessed via a web interface or REST API, enabling mobile app development.

- **Free Trial:** RYTR's free trial availability is unknown, and OpenAI offers a limited free trial for the GPT-3 API.
- **Monthly Price:** RYTR's monthly price is unclear, and GPT-3 API pricing depends on the use case and usage amount.

RYTR and ChatGPT produce high-quality output for their intended tasks. RYTR may have an advantage in generating text with specific styles or tones, while ChatGPT delivers consistently high-quality output across a wide range of language tasks.

8. Poe by Quora: A ChatGPT Alternative for Social Media

Launched in early 2023, Poe by Quora is not an AI chatbot itself but rather a platform where users can interact with various AI bots. As an acronym for "Platform for Open Exploration," Quora Poe stays true to its name, providing a space for users to engage in conversations and experiment with a diverse range of AI-powered chatbots.

Contrary to any concerns, Poe is not a chatbot that utilizes question-answer data from Quora. The platform is neatly designed and currently enables users to communicate with AI bots such as Sage, ChatGPT, Dragonfly, and even the more advanced GPT-4 and Claude+. However, access to the latter two is limited to one message per day.

Quora Poe functions efficiently with minimal downtime as users converse with the various AI bots. To access the platform, users must create an account, but the upside is that a single account grants access to all the available services. An iOS app is also available, although there is no Android app at this time.

For those who enjoy using ChatGPT-like tools but prefer a centralized platform to access them, Poe can be the ideal all-in-one solution.

ChatGPT vs. Poe by Quora

Poe, which stands for "Platform for Open Exploration," offers an exclusive iOS-based experience, providing access to a variety of conversational AI platforms. It's like having a messaging app designed specifically for AI models, allowing users to engage in thought-provoking discussions on Poe's chat platform, covering topics such as writing assistance and culinary exploration.

The driving force behind this ChatGPT alternative is a collaboration between OpenAI and Anthropic, according to Quora.

Let's delve into Poe's key features:

- Centralized access to multiple conversational AI platforms: Poe enables users to interact with various AI chatbots in one convenient location.
- Simplified integration with an upcoming API: Quora is developing an API to allow AI developers to easily connect their models to Poe, streamlining the user experience even further.
- Exclusive iOS availability: Poe can be found as an iOS app on the Apple Store.

Pricing for Poe:

Currently, Poe is accessible through its app, with no specific pricing information available. While Poe is an excellent platform, it may not surpass Chatsonic in terms of features and usability. If you find yourself torn between the two, Chatsonic is the recommended choice for a well-rounded experience!

Bottom Line

I hope this list of ChatGPT alternatives proves valuable when you need an alternative during downtimes. There's no shortage of AI chatbots on the market. Interestingly, even Elon Musk, Twitter's CEO, is planning to develop his own ChatGPT alternative. Rumor has it that he's reaching out to Igor Babuschkin, a former DeepMind researcher, for collaboration. If successful, Musk's creation will directly compete with OpenAI, a company he co-founded. Musk should ensure his offering provides extensive data access, as ChatGPT now has Internet connectivity, giving it a significant advantage. Once you've explored these options, consider checking out the best AI art generators for a creative visual experience or deepfake apps and websites for unique visual content creation.

If you're seeking the most comprehensive ChatGPT alternative, consider incorporating ChatSonic into your toolkit. It enhances ChatGPT's capabilities by providing a suite of writing tools. For seasoned content creators and marketing professionals, Jasper AI can accelerate your workflow while maintaining quality, and its Jasper Chat feature offers a robust conversational AI solution. To sum it up, AI and machine learning technologies are quickly becoming ubiquitous, and it's reassuring to know that reliable alternatives and innovative approaches to well-established platforms like ChatGPT are readily available.

Conclusion

"Success is not final; failure is not fatal; it is the courage to continue that counts." Winston Churchill

As we conclude our journey through the "ChatGPT Money Guide," let us remember this quote, which encapsulates the essence of what we've learned together. By preparing ourselves with the right knowledge and tools, we can seize the opportunities that ChatGPT presents for generating income and achieving financial success.

Throughout this guide, we've covered a wide range of topics that have provided you with essential insights, strategies, and tips for unlocking the full potential of ChatGPT. Now, let's take a moment to reflect on the key ingredients we've explored, and how they can help you transform your content creation and marketing efforts.

Setting the Foundations for Financial Success

A solid foundation is vital for long-term success in any venture. We began our journey by discussing the importance of setting clear financial goals, understanding your target audience, and honing your time management skills. By mastering these fundamentals, you're better equipped to embark on a successful career, leveraging ChatGPT as a powerful tool to boost your income potential.

Making Money with Content Creation That You Need to Know

Content is king, and in today's digital landscape, it's more important than ever to create high-quality, engaging content that stands out from the competition. We delved into the essential skills and strategies required to thrive in the content creation industry, including understanding SEO, keyword research, and crafting compelling headlines.

By harnessing the power of ChatGPT, you can automate the process of generating creative and unique content, significantly increasing your productivity and output. This enables you to take on more projects, grow your client base, and ultimately, generate more income.

Level Up Your Content Marketing with ChatGPT

A successful content marketing strategy is essential for driving traffic, generating leads, and increasing sales. We explored how ChatGPT can streamline your content marketing efforts by producing high-quality, optimized content that resonates with your target audience. By utilizing AI-generated content, you can save time, reduce the cost of content production, and ensure a consistent and effective message across all marketing channels.

Moreover, ChatGPT can help you identify trends and topics that are relevant to your audience, allowing you to create content that addresses their needs and preferences. This not only boosts engagement but also increases the likelihood of your content being shared, further expanding your reach and potential revenue streams.

How ChatGPT is Changing the Social Media Marketing Game

Social media has become an indispensable tool for businesses and individuals alike, providing a platform for connecting with audiences and promoting products and services. We examined how ChatGPT is revolutionizing social media marketing by generating captivating, shareable content that grabs attention and encourages engagement.

By leveraging ChatGPT's capabilities, you can create a consistent, powerful social media presence that strengthens your brand's reputation and drives traffic to your website or online store. The result is increased conversions, customer loyalty, and ultimately higher revenue.

How To Increase Productivity with ChatGPT As A Freelancer

Freelancing offers flexibility, autonomy, and the potential for a lucrative income. However, it also comes with challenges, such as time management and maintaining a steady flow of clients. We discussed how ChatGPT can help freelancers overcome these hurdles by automating time-consuming tasks and generating high-quality content that meets client expectations.

By incorporating ChatGPT into your workflow, you can focus on acquiring new clients, expanding your skillset, and nurturing relationships with existing clients. This ultimately leads to a more stable and successful freelance career, allowing you to enjoy the benefits of working on your own terms.

ChatGPT and its Alternatives

The AI landscape is constantly evolving, and it's essential to stay informed about the various tools and platforms available. We considered ChatGPT and its alternatives, weighing the pros and cons of each to help you make an informed decision about which AI tool best suits your needs. By familiarizing yourself with different AI-powered solutions, you can stay ahead of the curve and adapt your strategies as the industry evolves.

Now, as we reach the conclusion of this guide, it's time for you to take action. You've gained valuable insights into how ChatGPT can revolutionize your content creation and marketing efforts, helping you generate income quickly and easily. Don't let this newfound knowledge go to waste. Put it to good use and start capitalizing on the opportunities that ChatGPT presents.

So, embrace the power of ChatGPT and begin integrating it into your workflow today. Explore its features, experiment with different strategies, and fine-tune your approach to maximize its potential. Remember, the key to success lies in preparation and seizing opportunities. With ChatGPT by your side, you're well equipped to do just that.

As you embark on this exciting journey, keep the friendly tone of this guide in mind. Be open to collaboration, share your experiences with others, and learn from the successes and challenges of your peers. By fostering a supportive community around ChatGPT, we can all grow together and enjoy the financial rewards that come with mastering this powerful AI tool.

So go forth, and let ChatGPT be your catalyst for financial success. The world of content creation and marketing is ever-changing, and with the right tools and strategies, you can not only adapt to these changes but also thrive in the face of them. Start today and unlock the potential of ChatGPT to transform your income and achieve the financial success you've always dreamed of.

Ready, set, ChatGPT! Tap into your inner wordsmith and unlock the secret to a thriving and rewarding career.

Leave a Review

Thank you so much for purchasing my book!

Before you go, I wanted to ask you for one small favor, as an independent author with a small marketing budget, reviews are my livelihood on this platform. **Could you please consider posting a review on the platform?**

If you enjoyed this book, I'd really appreciate it if you left your honest feedback. I love hearing from my readers and I personally read every single review.

Your feedback will help me to keep writing the kind of books that will help you get the results you want. It would mean a lot to me to hear from you.